Best of
ROSANNE CASH

Photo © Abby Ross

ISBN 978-1-61780-333-8

HAL•LEONARD® CORPORATION

7777 W. BLUEMOUND RD. P.O. BOX 13819 MILWAUKEE, WI 53213

In Australia Contact:
Hal Leonard Australia Pty. Ltd.
4 Lentara Court
Cheltenham, Victoria, 3192 Australia
Email: ausadmin@halleonard.com.au

Visit Hal Leonard Online at
www.halleonard.com

Visit Notable Music Online at
www.notablemusic.net

When first learning how to write a song, you aren't necessarily aware that that's what you're doing, anymore than a small child compelled to crawl towards a shiny object is consciously aware that he or she is learning to mobilize on behalf of desire. There is a hunger that makes the dirty business of learning—the striving and failing—inconsequential. You merely hold the silvery picture in your mind's eye of the way you might possess Song, and in turn, how it will wholly possess you. And then it is slowly pulled into your being like oxygen from blood: there for the taking, dead without it.

As we go on, the great desire for most songwriters is to be seduced—by story and character, by rhythm, tension, and resolve; by words seeking animation; by wild notions so thick with the romance of possibility that they seem almost to conjure themselves into existence, and us along with them. Our very identity is at stake, then, and so we push urgently, naively forward, until a new language begins to take shape in our mouths simultaneous to thought… until a language of expression becomes so persuasive, in fact, as to form our thoughts. We feel something unexpected and lyrical leave our tongues and decide to follow. Then we write the next verse to affirm and extend the first, whatever it might mean, and wherever it might be taking us. We write—almost all of us—not to express what we know and love and believe, but to discover it.

It makes of us twitchy and desperate companions… unfit company for others save more of our own kind. And we are sorry for that, I will tell you, until we aren't anymore… until that third verse finally arrives to make all things, once again, romantic with possibility.

Rosanne Cash grew up within a tradition of desperate singers and heroic songs. The rural southern music that is a part of her familial and creative heritage was a convention thick with lovers, traitors, killers, redeemers, and blasphemers—either hiding or confessing, but all with their savage, glorious humanity on display.

Rosanne crawled toward the shiny object of that humanity, passed through it and emerged having absorbed its familiar tone and structure; but as well, the influence of young musical upstarts like The Beatles and Bob Dylan, Joni Mitchell, Neil Young, and a host of rangy west coasters who stood just ahead of her in years. She has arrived at a most singular juncture that finds the broader tradition of American song bending to meet her, transfiguring it all into something new, introspective and intensely personal.

Yet the more intimately she speaks from her own experience, the more she seems to illuminate the beating hearts of the rest of us. Rosanne understands and employs the mysterious language of poetry, but a great song is not a failed poem, not a stepchild. It operates from a distinct dynamic plane, because sound itself has meaning, and because a song is never finished, as it is forever being reinvented. That's what separates song from the rest of literature: each time it is taken up, a song is like a genie rising out of a lamp, asking who you are and what you might need of it this time. It animates language and sends it into the air to make a living thing out of it. Where written words provoke thought, a song can make it jump and flicker within us like a movie projected against the curved back wall of your mind's eye. Rosanne's songs invariably engage emotional struggle, but never in a vacuum: heartbreak doesn't happen without the possibility of love's reclamation, and death is not the end; and I never feel she walks me into either alone. Her flickering light is, for me, always conspiratorial, always shared in answer to darkness.

As a songwriter, Rosanne is perhaps less a narrative storyteller and more an emotionally adept revealer. And what she reveals with great clarity is the dense mystery of living's true nature: song after song, she invites us to see that love connects us and fear divides us—simply, confoundingly, inescapably; and that life, yes, when taken up, is always and forever being reinvented.

Rosanne Cash stands alone, finally, as a songwriter and a singer—apart from any others to whom by name she might always be attached; finally, but not Finally. Songs are things in flux, after all, and in motion. And Rose is still moving along with them.

Joe Henry
November, 2010

CONTENTS

© Ethan Russell

© Sam Rayner

© Sam Rayner

© Deborah Feingold

CASH

BLUE MOON WITH HEARTACHE

Words and Music by
ROSANNE CASH

Slow Country feeling

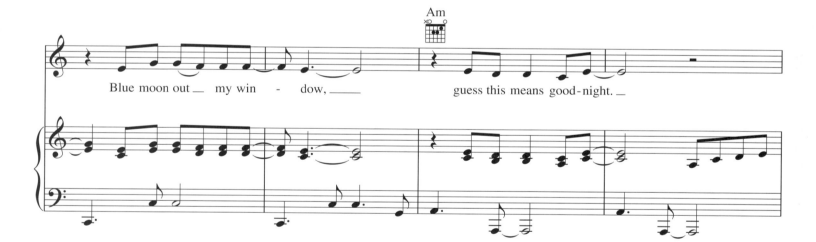

Blue moon out __ my win - dow, ___ guess this means good-night. __

Then you come in __ and start __ right in __ not treat-in' me right.

Recorded a half step lower.

Well, mis-er-y's a bore ___ and _____ and all its com - pa-ny,

I'll play the vic-tim for _____ you hon-ey, but not for __ free.

I run in-to that heart-ache _____ just _____ like a __ wall,

and act like __ noth-in' hap-pened to ___ me, noth-in' at all.

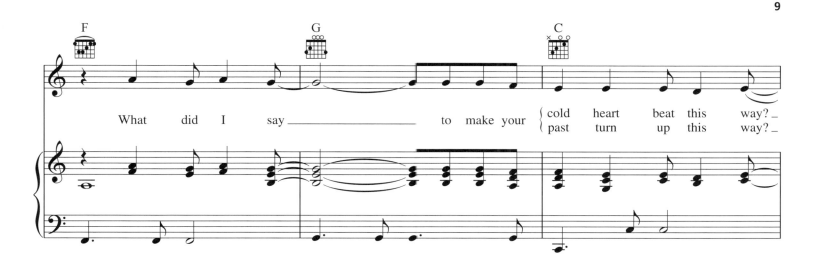

What did I say _____ to make your {cold heart beat this way?_ {past turn up this way?_

May-be I'll just go a-way___ to-

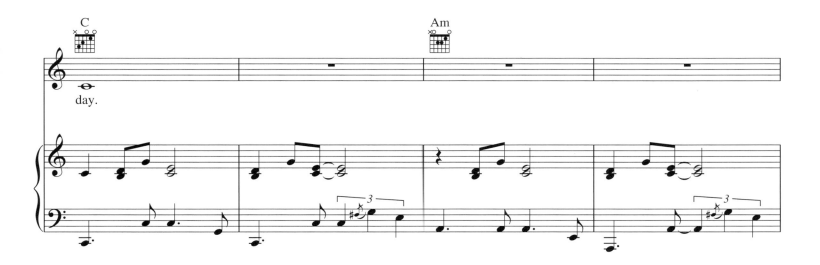

day.

And I don't care___ who's wait - in'___ at my

front door._____ You know that life don't hold___

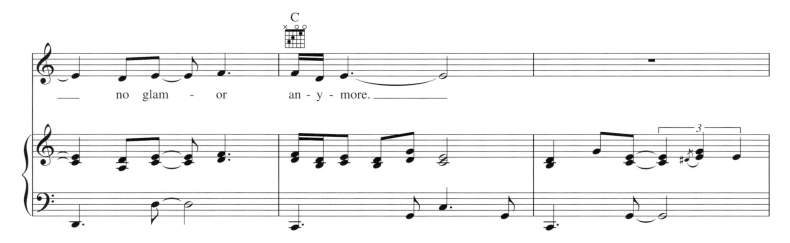

___ no glam - or an - y - more._____

How can it all look so right___ and feel___ so wrong._____

11

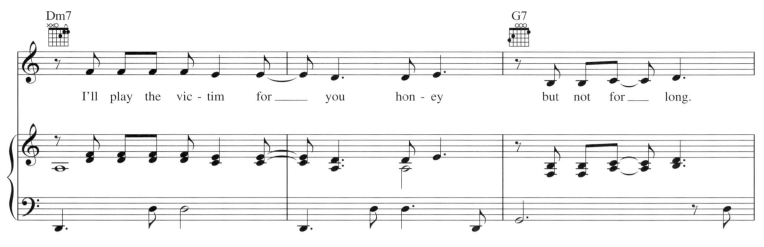

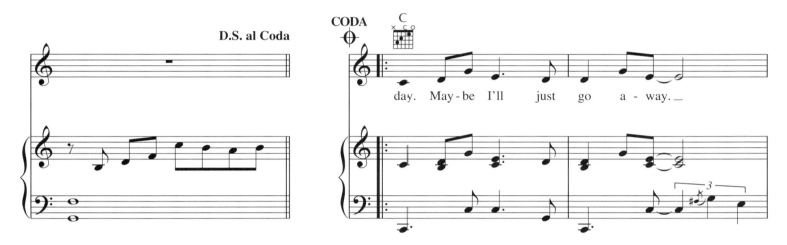

DREAMS ARE NOT MY HOME

Words and Music by
ROSANNE CASH

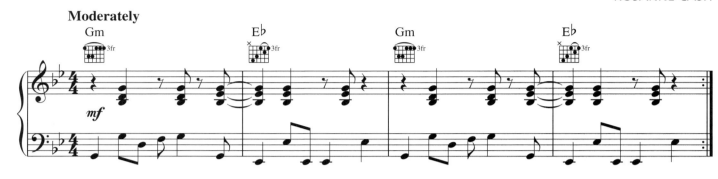

The waves are break-ing _____ on the wall. _____

The queen of ros-es _____ spreads her arms _____

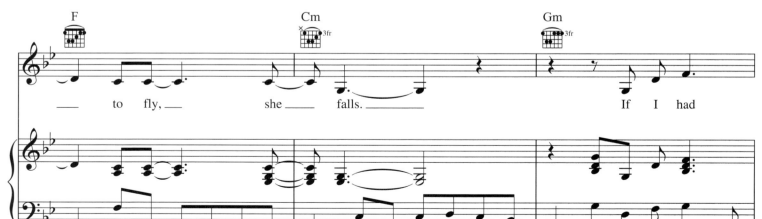

to fly, _____ she _____ falls. _____ If I had

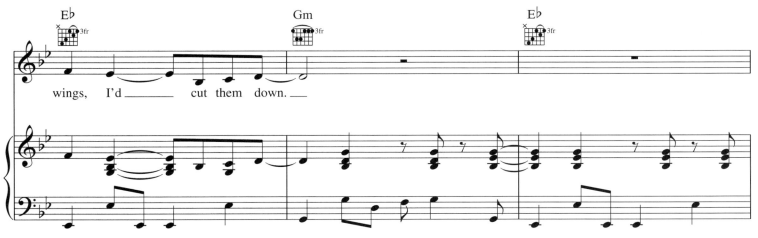

girl. I wan-na know _____ I'm not a-lone _____ and that dreams ___

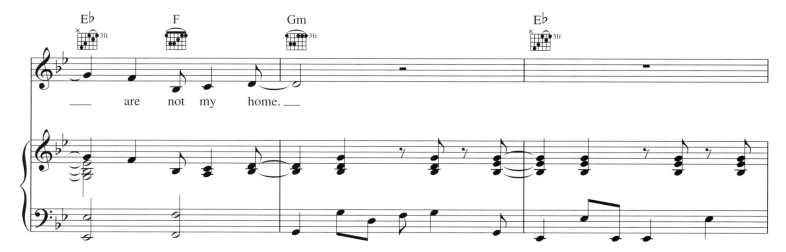

___ are not my home. ___

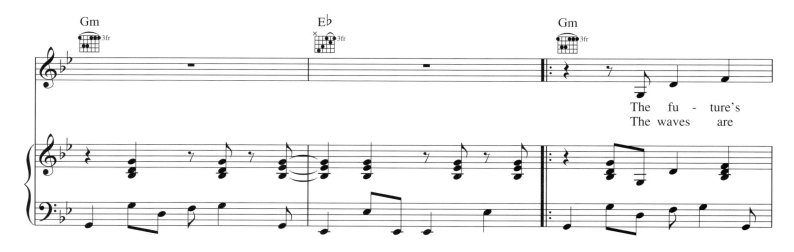

The fu-ture's
The waves are

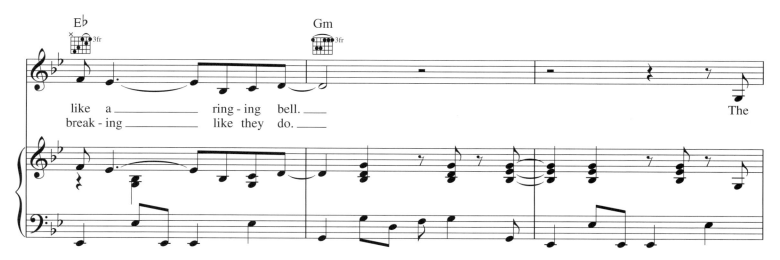

like a _____ ring-ing bell. ___
break-ing _____ like they do. ___

The

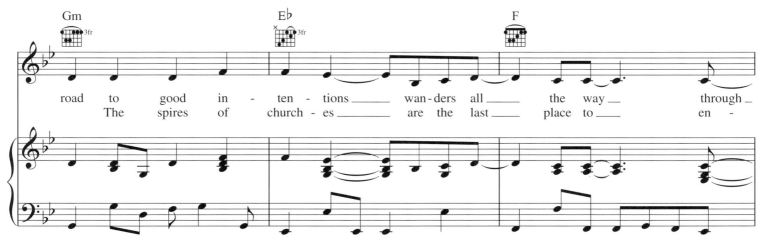

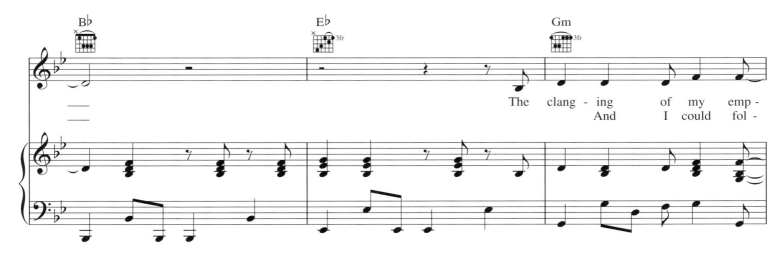

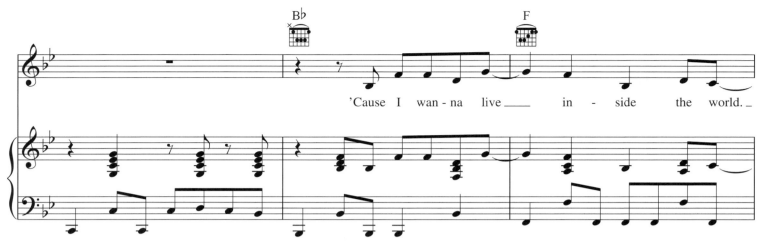

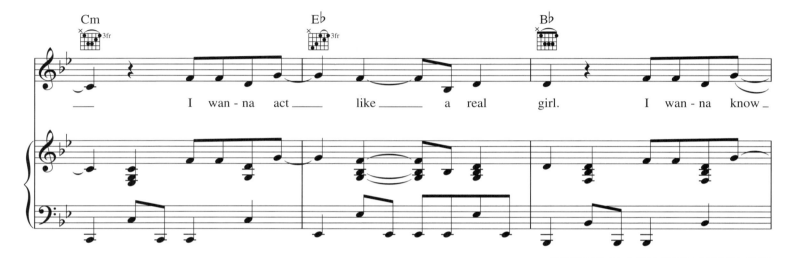

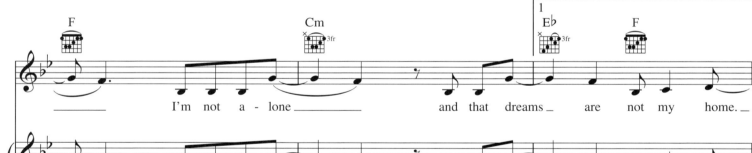

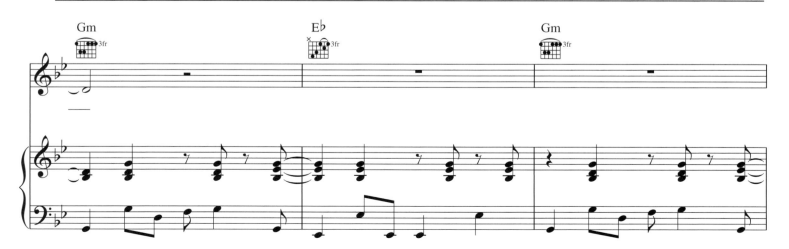

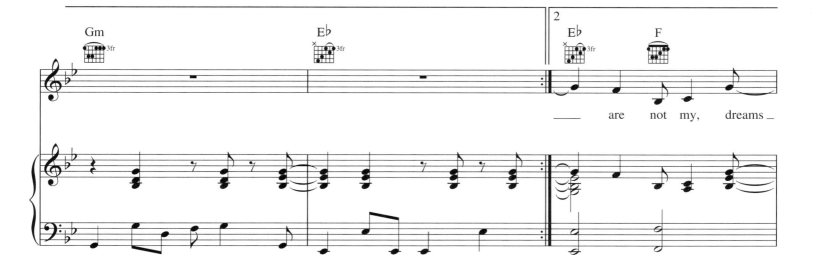

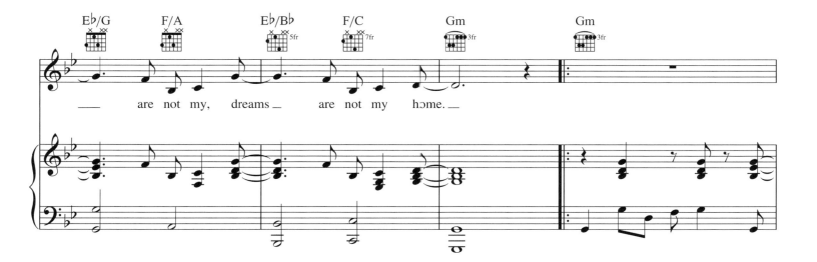

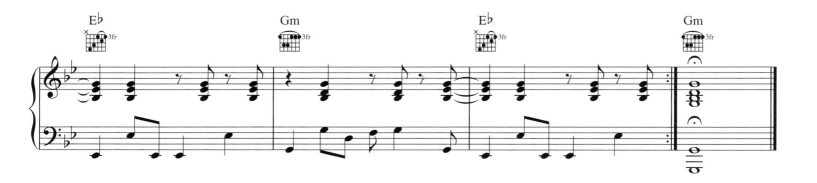

THE GOOD INTENT

Words and Music by ROSANNE CASH
and JOHN LEVENTHAL

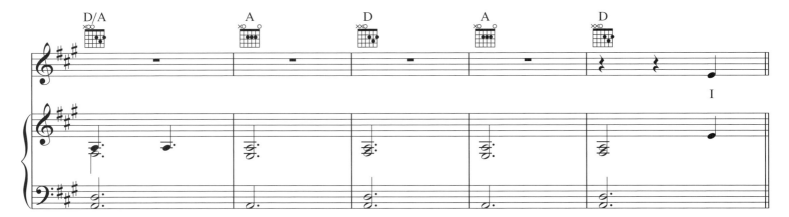

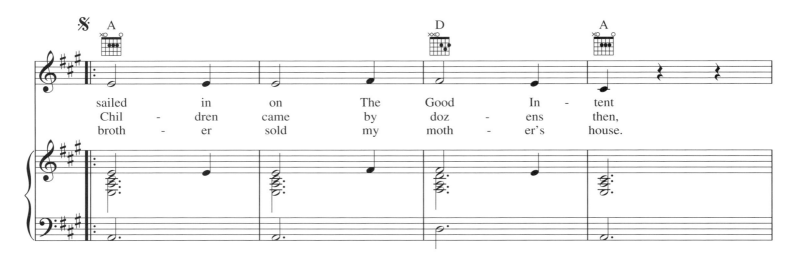

sailed in on The Good In - tent then,
Chil - dren came by doz - ens then,
broth - er came sold my moth - er's house.

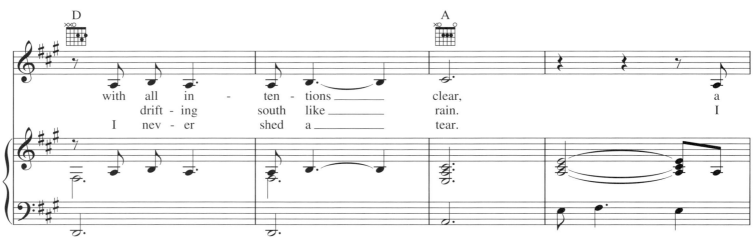

with all in - ten - tions _____ clear,   a
drift - ing south like _____ rain.   I
I nev - er shed a _____ tear.

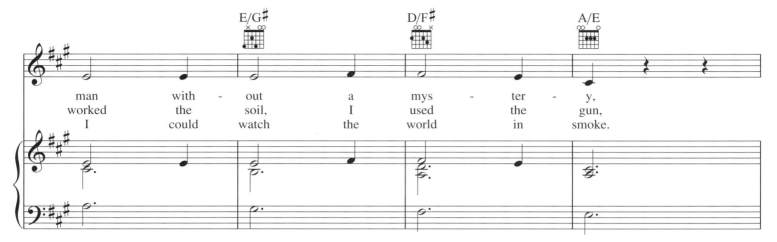

man with- out a mys- ter- y,
worked the soil, I used the gun,
I could watch the world in smoke.

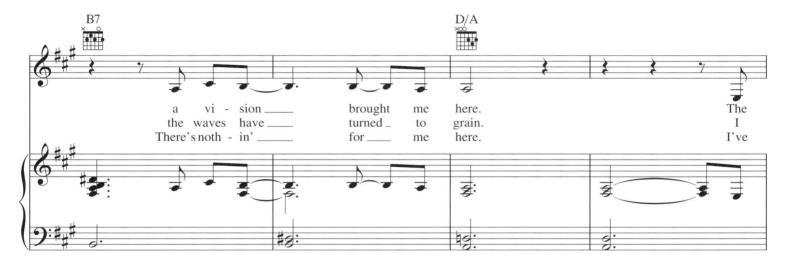

a vi- sion _____ brought me here. The
the waves have _____ turned to grain. I
There's noth- in' _____ for _____ me here. I've

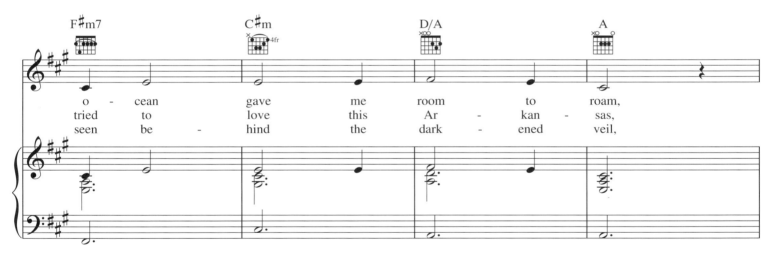

o- cean gave me room to roam,
tried to love this Ar- kan- sas,
seen be- hind the dark- ened veil,

but the shore is call- ing out. So,
with black and bleed- ing hands. But
that's all I want to know. So, I'll

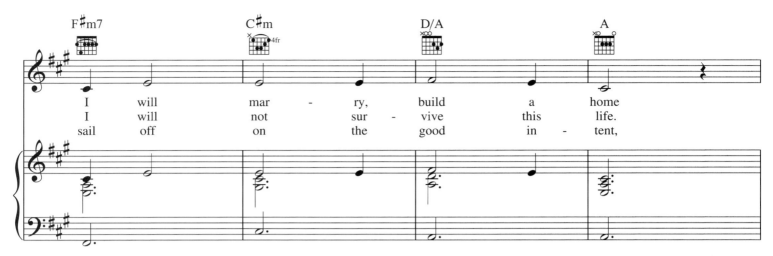

I will mar - ry, build a home
I will not sur - vive this life.
sail off on the good in - tent,

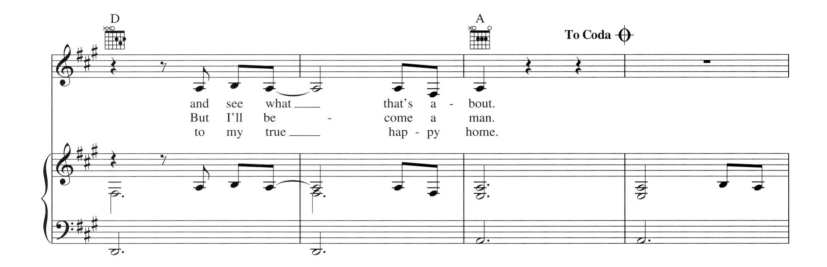

and see what ____ that's a - bout.
But I'll be - come a man.
to my true ____ hap - py home.

To Coda ⊕

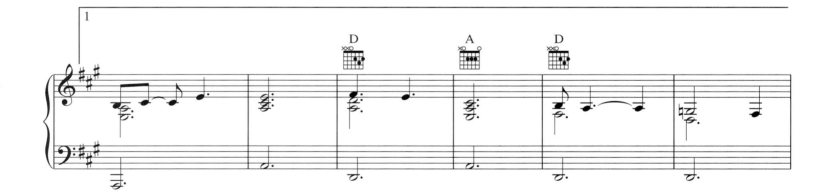

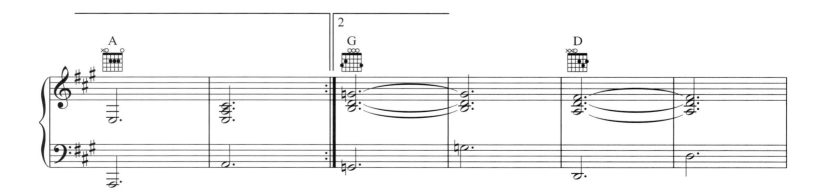

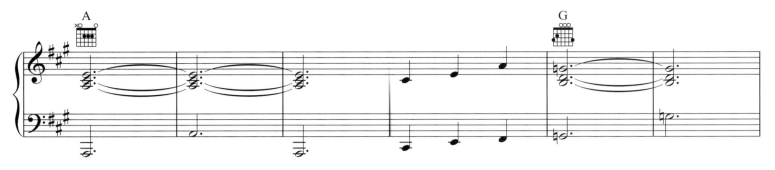

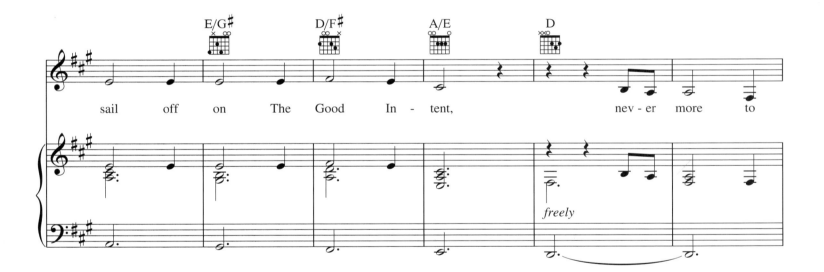

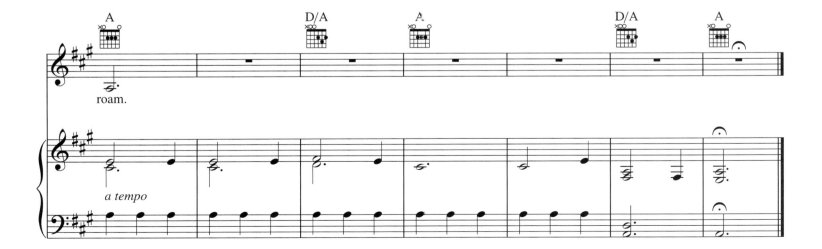

HOLD ON

Words and Music by
ROSANNE CASH

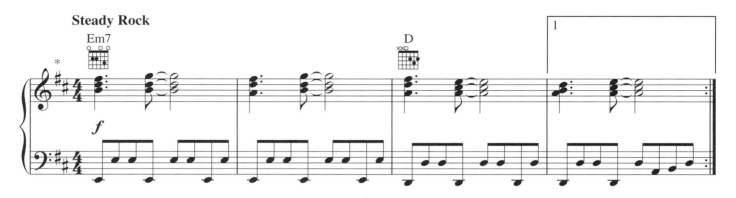

Steady Rock

Lyrics:

If you want to keep _____ a wom-an like me, ___ you got to
you want to know _____ how far we can go, ___ you got to
you think you need _____ a wom-an like me, ___ you got to

hold on. _____ If you want to see _____ how
hold on. _____ If you take it slow, ___ then I got
hold on. _____ If you want to find ___ what I got ___

Recorded a half step lower.

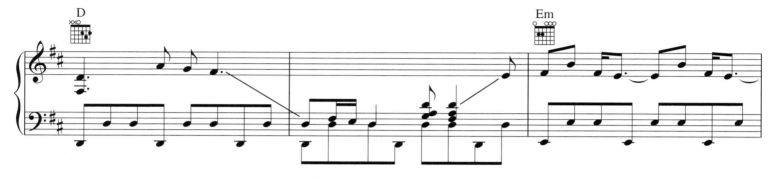

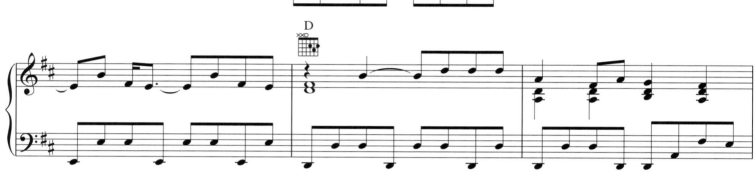

She'll give you rea-sons for her ___ kind; you might be-lieve it, but I'm ___

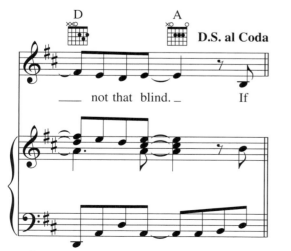

D.S. al Coda

___ not that blind. ___ If

CODA

hold on. ___ If

you want to keep _____ a wom-an like me, _____ ba-by, hold on. ____

You've got to

Repeat and Fade

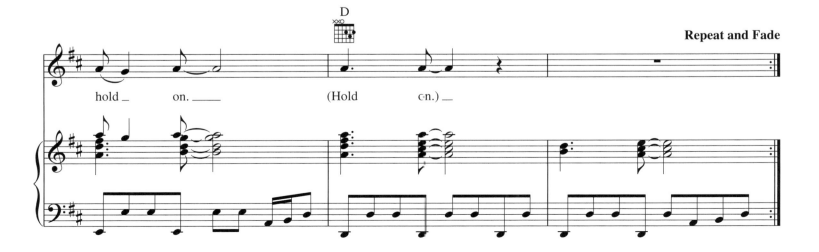

hold __ on. ____ (Hold on.) __

I DON'T KNOW WHY YOU DON'T WANT ME

Words and Music by ROSANNE CASH
and RODNEY CROWELL

night. _____ I'm in the right mood _ I've got my
(I don't know why you don't want me.)

new shoes _____ to - night. _____ I've got my
(I don't know why you don't

new dress _ I could-n't hurt less _____ to - night. _____
want me.)

I don't know why you don't want me.   Some-bod - y told _ you

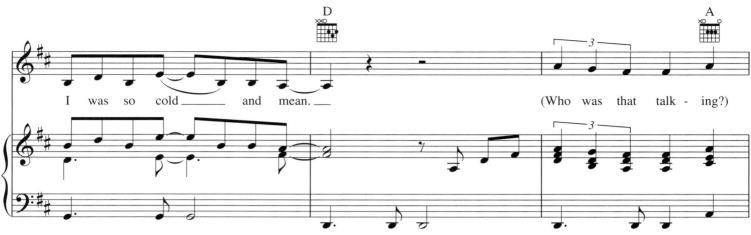

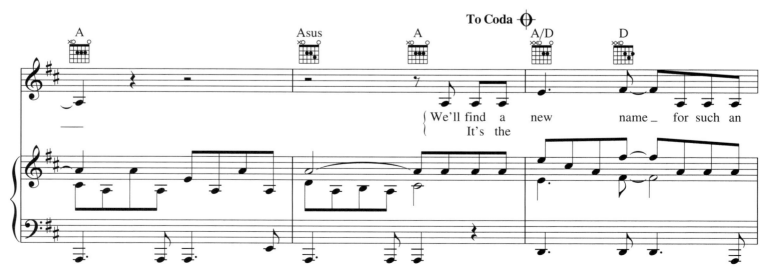

old   game _____ to - night. _____

I'll show you
(I don't know why   you don't

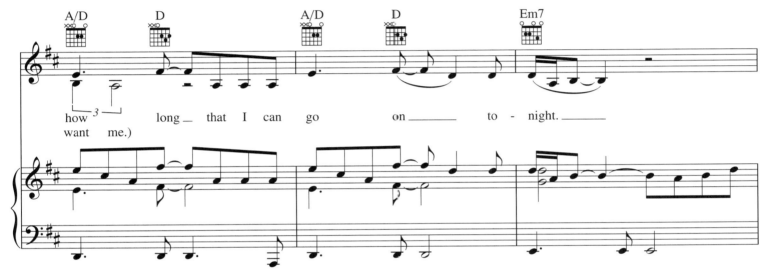

how ³_____ long __ that I can go   on _____ to - night. _____
want me.)

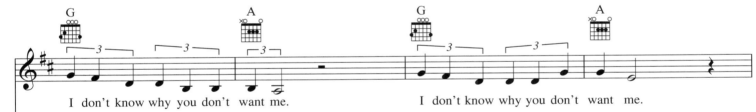

I don't know why you don't want me.   I don't know why you don't want me.

Just when I think __ that I can make it with-out you,   you come a - round __ and say you want me   now. __ You

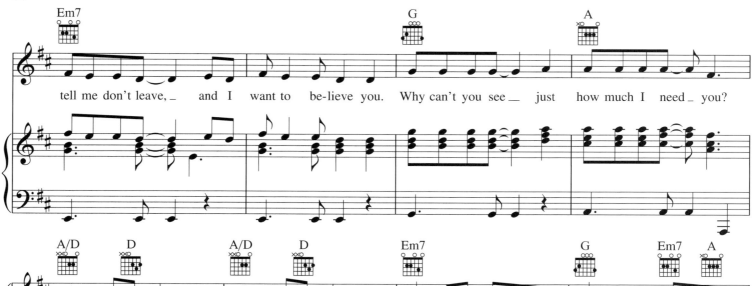

tell me don't leave, _ and I want to be-lieve you. Why can't you see _ just how much I need _ you?

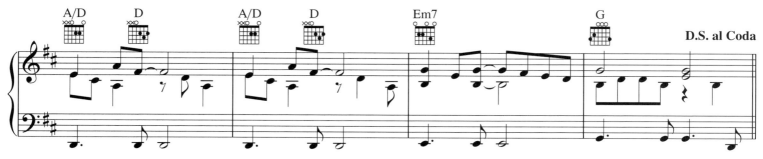

D.S. al Coda

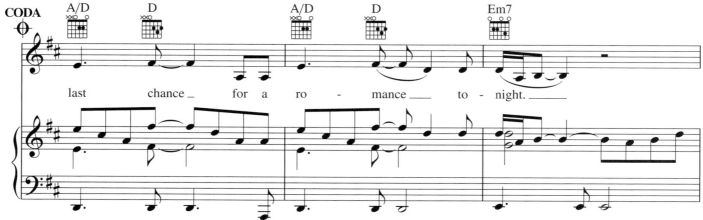

CODA

last chance _ for a ro - mance ____ to - night. ____

There'll be no next time _ if you won't be mine ____ to -
(I don't know why you don't want me.)

I'LL CHANGE FOR YOU

Words and Music by
ROSANNE CASH

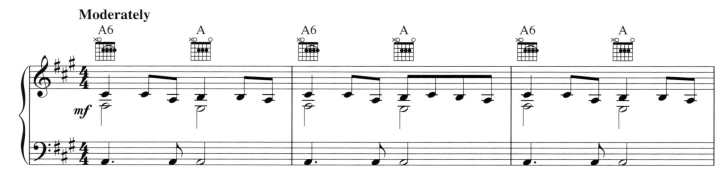

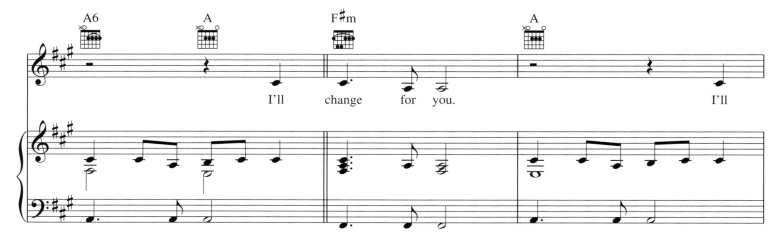

I'll change for you.   I'll

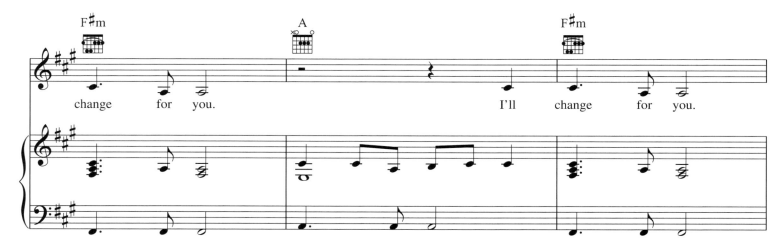

change for you.   I'll change for you.

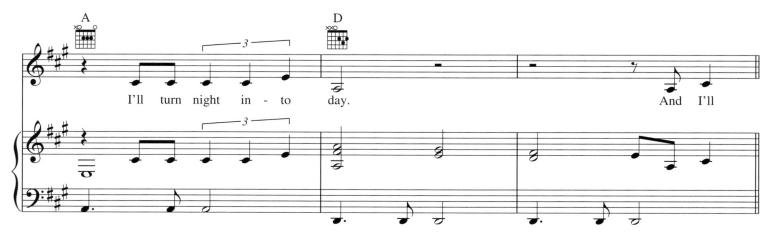

I'll turn night in-to day.   And I'll

change for you. *(spoken:) I don't care what the books say.* Oh, I'll change for you.
change for you. *(spoken:) And all the rules that we learned.* I'll change for you.

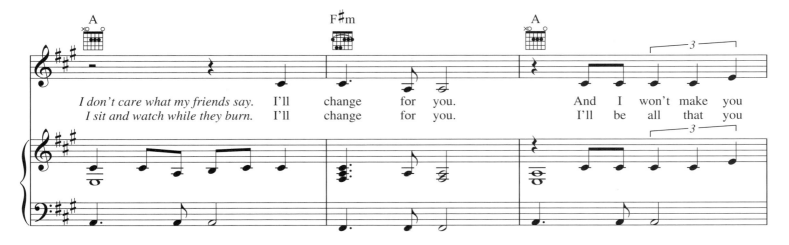

I don't care what my friends say. I'll change for you. And I won't make you
I sit and watch while they burn. I'll change for you. I'll be all that you

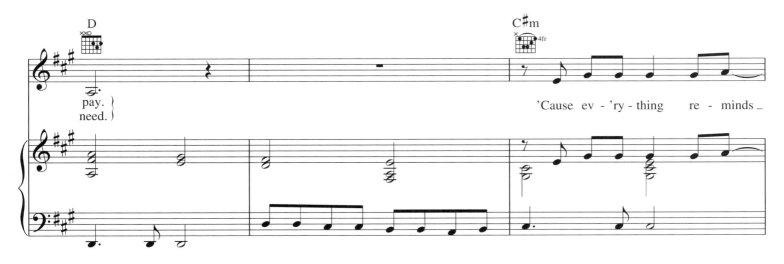

pay. }
need. }   'Cause ev - 'ry - thing re - minds _

_ me of you,   ba - by's feet, an old man's smile. _

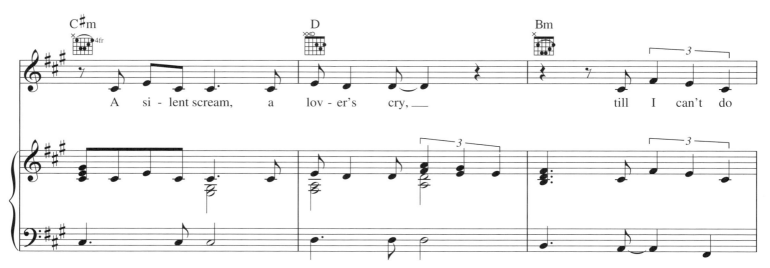

A si - lent scream, a lov - er's cry, ___ till I can't do

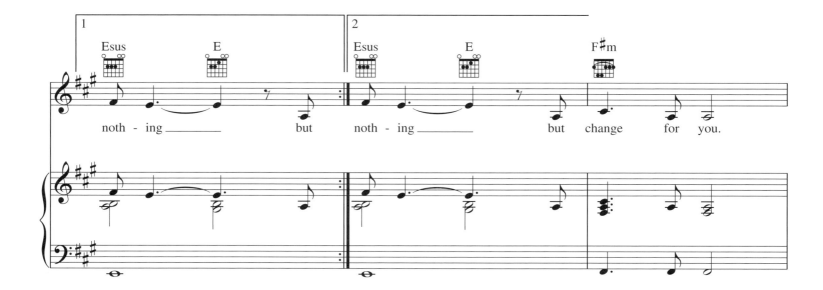

noth - ing _____ but noth - ing _____ but change for you.

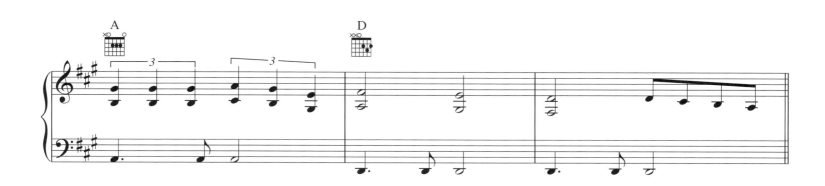

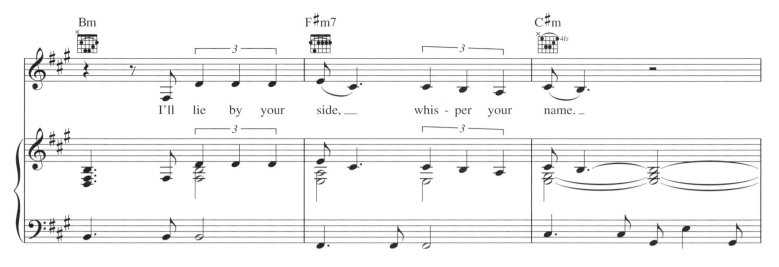

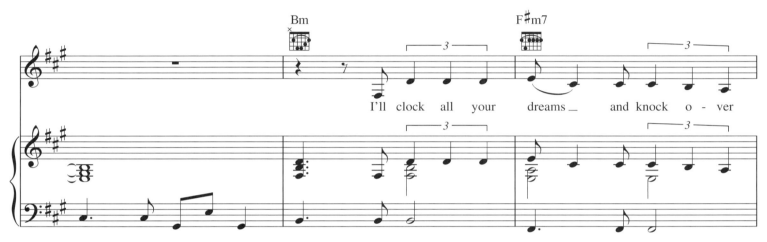

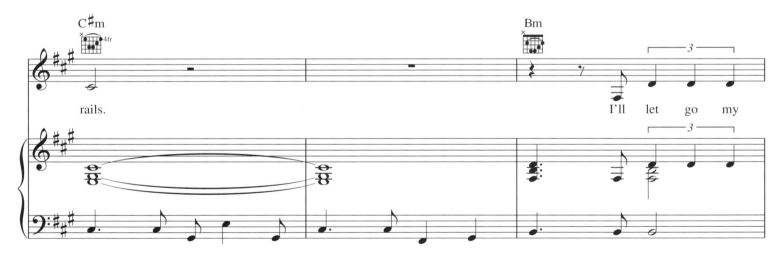

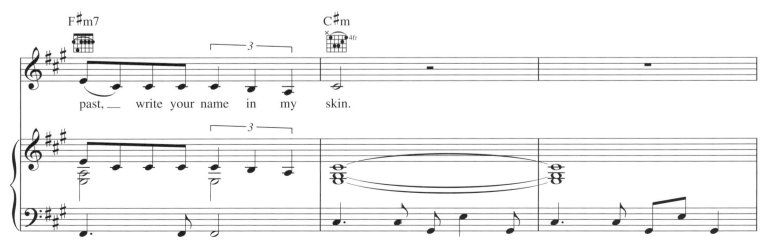

I'll trav - el through time to love you a - gain.

And I'll change for you. *I'll just wait for your word.* Oh, I'll

change for you. *And what you need I can learn.* I'll change for you.

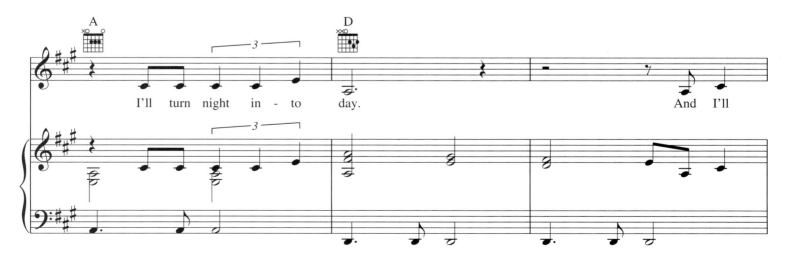

I'll turn night in - to day. And I'll

change for you. *And I'll give it my best.* I'll change for you. *And I won't stop till you rest.* I'll

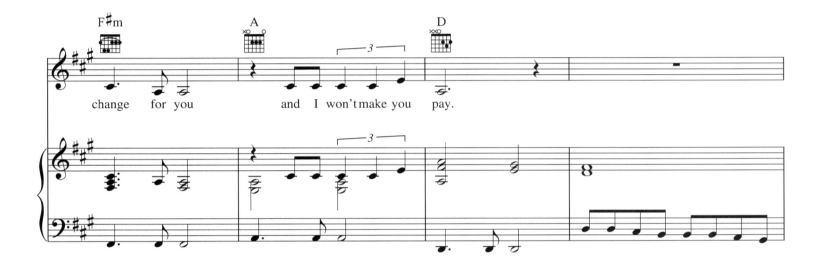

change for you and I won't make you pay.

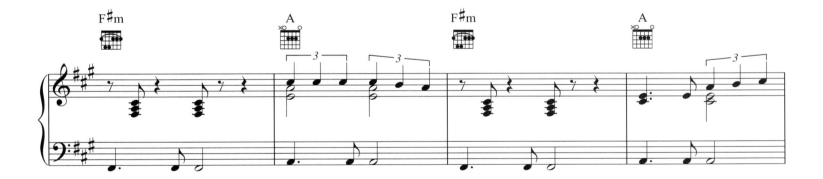

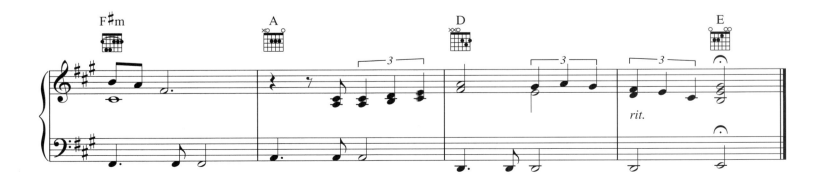

rit.

IF YOU CHANGE YOUR MIND

Words and Music by ROSANNE CASH
and HANK DeVITO

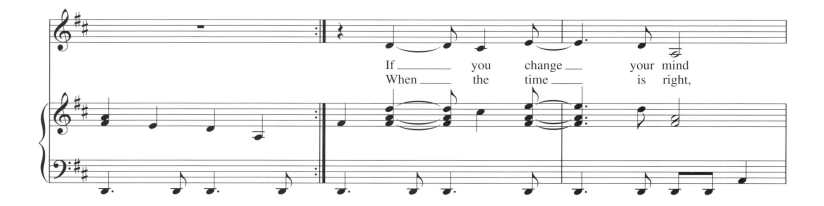

If ___ you change ___ your mind
When ___ the time ___ is right,

and leave ___ the past ___ be-hind,
I ___ can hold ___ you tight.

you ___ know
you ___ know

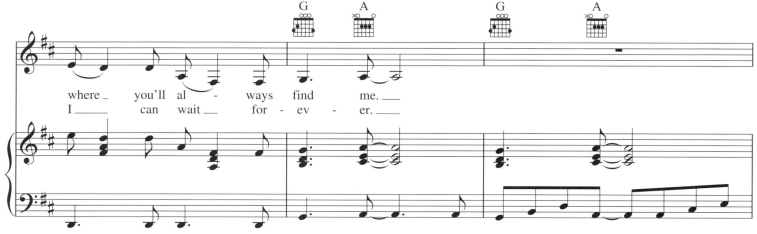

where ___ you'll al - ways find me. ___
I ___ can wait ___ for - ev - er. ___

And if _____ she breaks ___ your heart, and tears _____ your
And time _____ is on _____ our side. And we _____ can

world ___ a - part, you _____ can al - ways count ___ on ___
sure - ly find all _____ the love _____ we'll ev - er ___

D

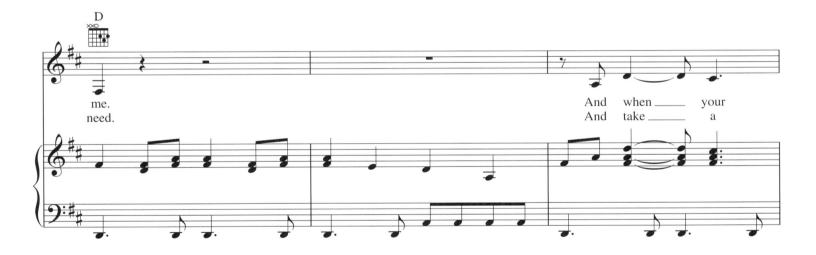

me. And when _____ your
need. And take _____ a

heart's ___ in doubt, and things _____ aren't work - ing out, ___
chance ___ on this. Seal _____ it with a kiss.

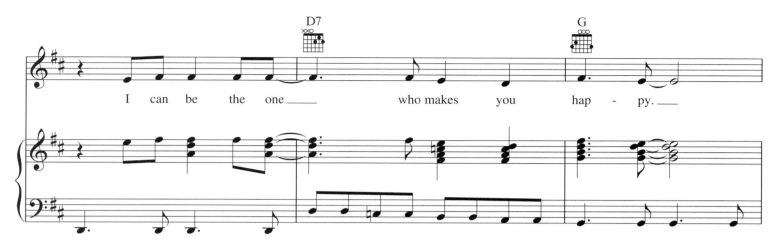

I can be the one ____ who makes you hap - py. ____

Call me on the tel - e - phone. ____

Dar - ling, I am ____ al - ways home ____ if ____ you

ev - er change ____ your mind.

mind.

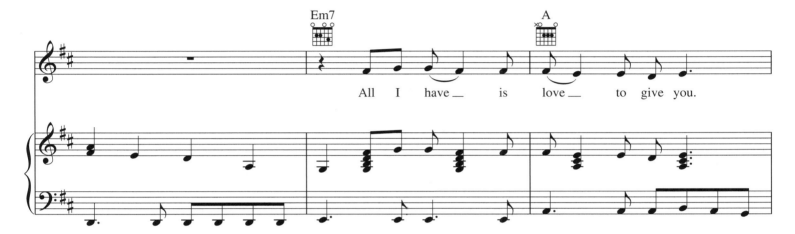

All I have __ is love __ to give you.

Ba - by, I could ___ be there __ with you if _____ you

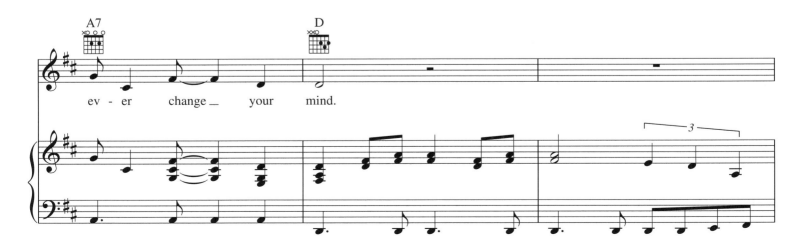

ev - er change __ your mind.

Call me on the tel - e - phone. _____ Dar - ling, I am _____

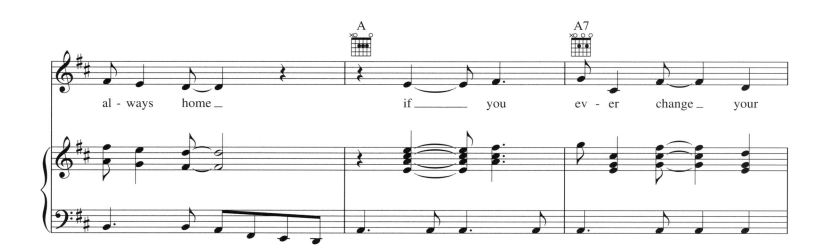

al - ways home _____ if _____ you ev - er change _____ your

mind.

WESTERN WALL

Words and Music by
ROSANNE CASH

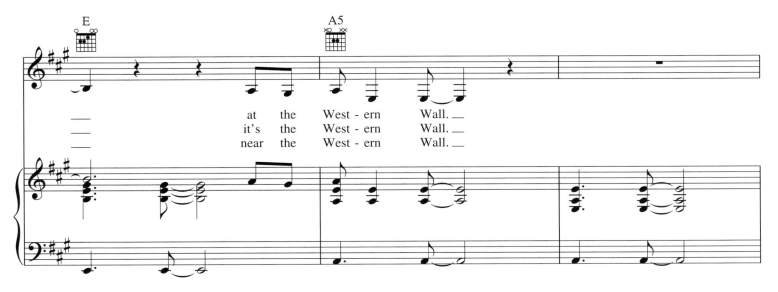

at the West - ern Wall. __
it's the West - ern Wall. __
near the West - ern Wall. __

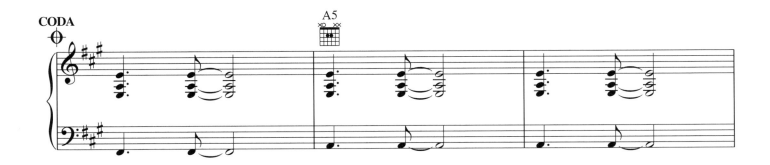

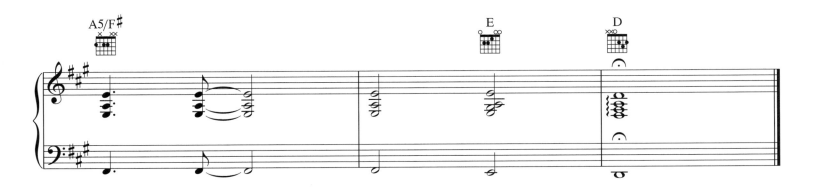

ON THE SURFACE

Words and Music by ROSANNE CASH
and JIMMY TITTLE

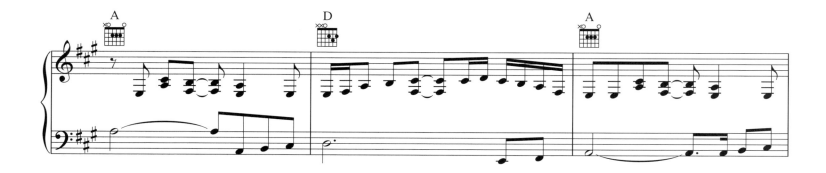

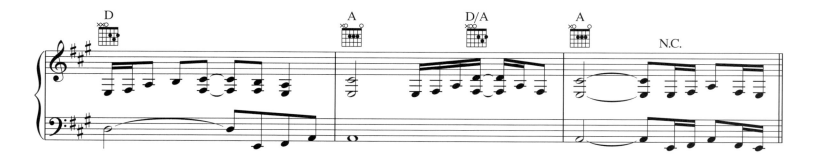

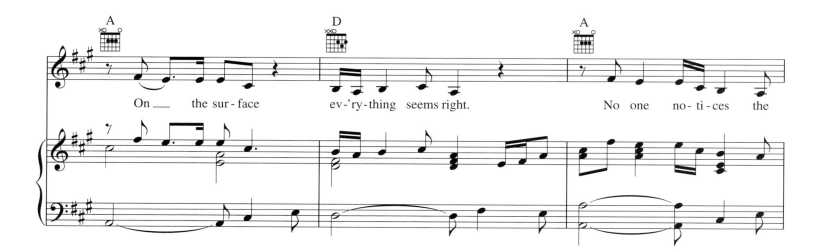

On __ the sur-face ev-'ry-thing seems right. No one no-ti-ces the

dim - ness of the light. For the world out - side our door __ our

smiles are oh so bright. __ On the sur - face ev - 'ry - thing's __ al -

right. We have the grace __ of act - ors on the stage. __

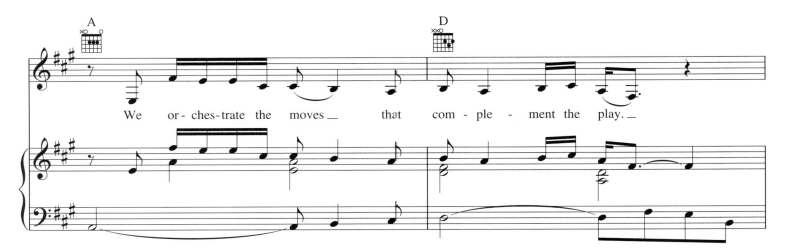

We or - ches - trate the moves __ that com - ple - ment the play. __

But the things that we be-lieve in, we just throw __ them a - way. __ And on the

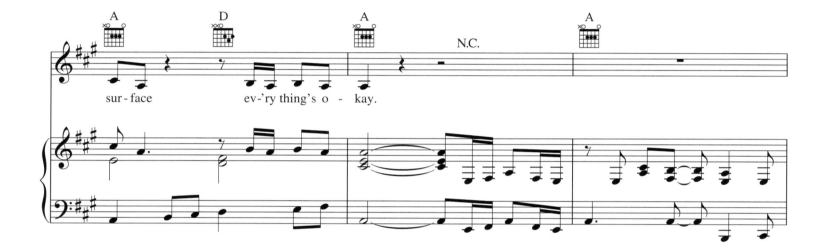

sur - face ev-'ry thing's o - kay.

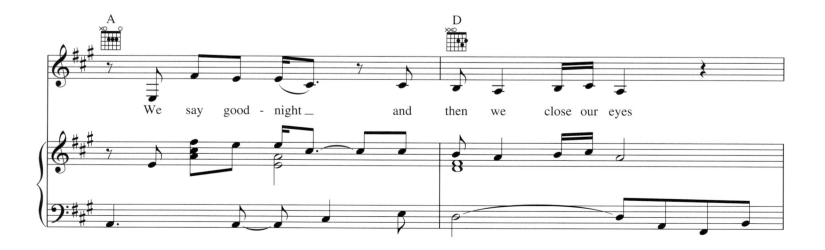

We say good - night __ and then we close our eyes

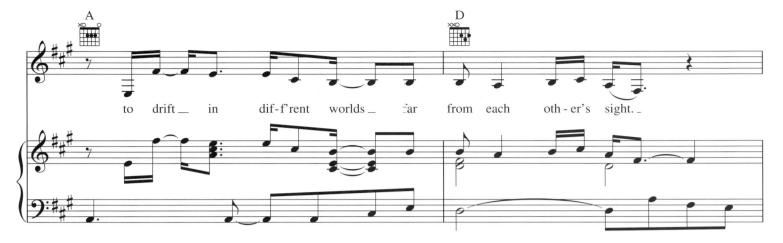

to drift __ in dif-f'rent worlds __ far from each oth-er's sight. __

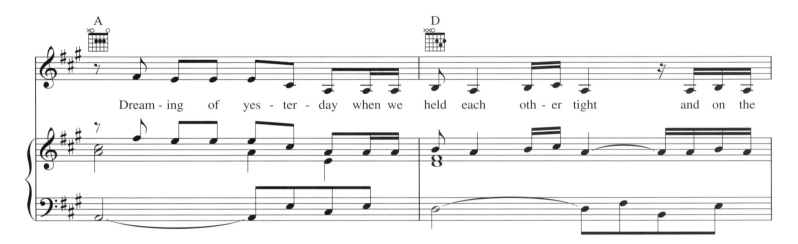

Dream-ing of yes-ter-day when we held each oth-er tight and on the

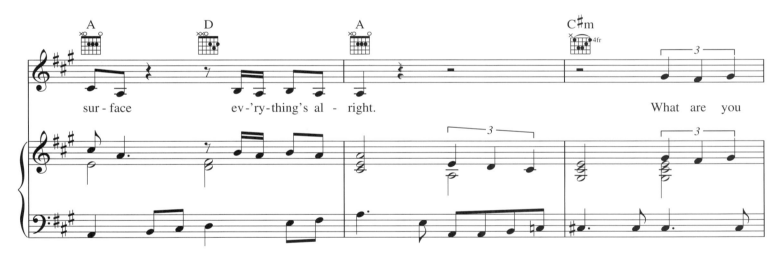

sur-face ev-'ry-thing's al - right. What are you

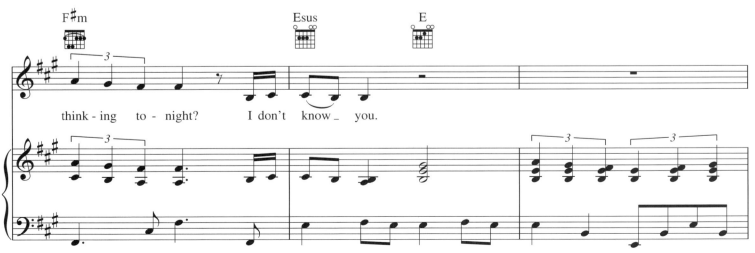

think-ing to-night? I don't know __ you.

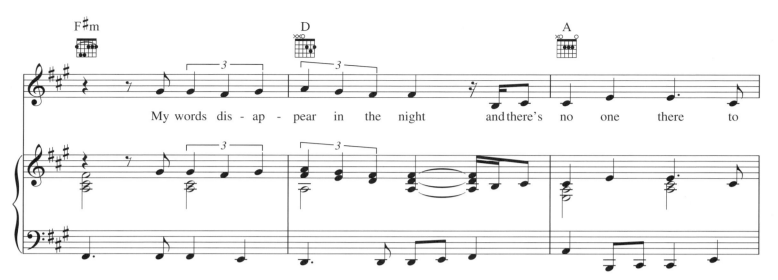

My words dis-ap-pear in the night and there's no one there to

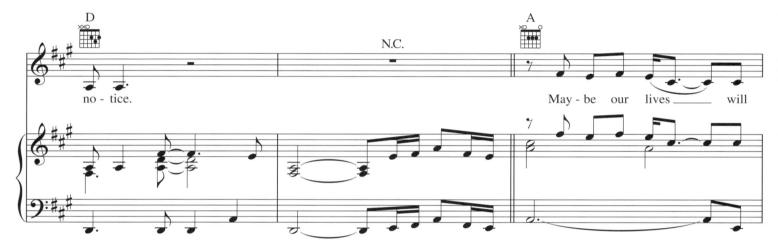

no-tice. May-be our lives _____ will

nev-er _____ be the same. _____ But we can face to-mor-row _____ if we can

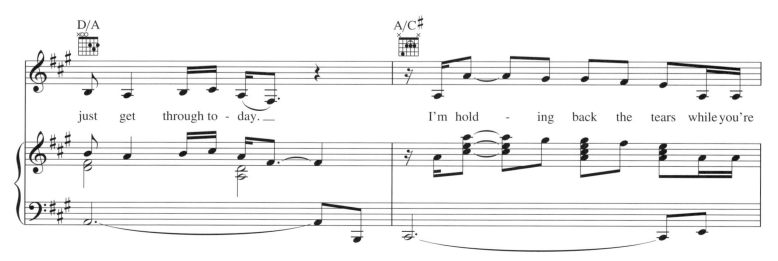

just get through to-day. _____ I'm hold-ing back the tears while you're

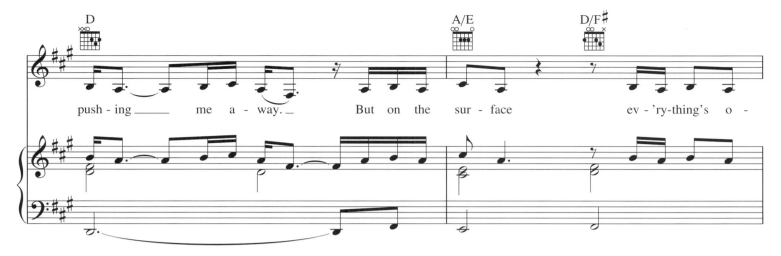

push-ing _____ me a - way. _____ But on the sur - face _____ ev - 'ry-thing's o -

kay. Yeah, on the sur - face ev - 'ry-thing's o - kay.

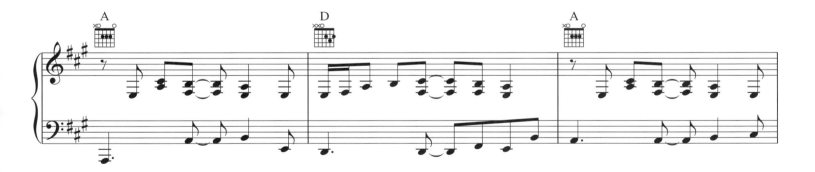

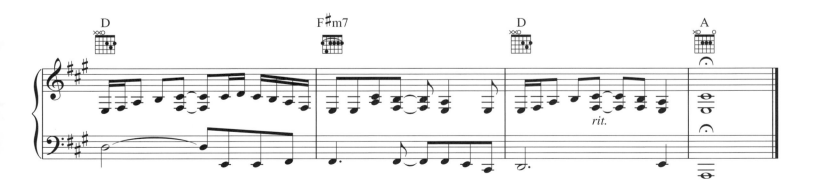

THE REAL ME

Words and Music by
ROSANNE CASH

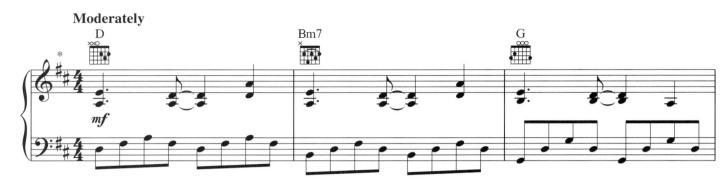

Recorded a half step lower.

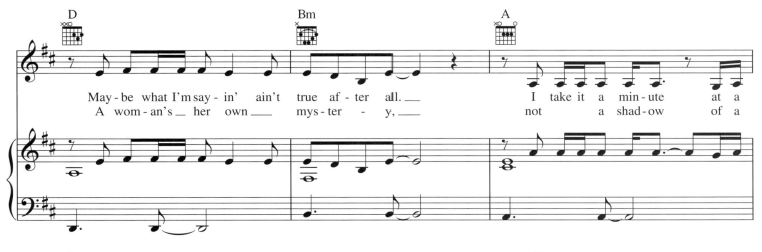

Maybe what I'm sayin' ain't true after all. ___ I take it a min-ute at a
A wom-an's ___ her own ___ mys-ter - y, ___ not a shad-ow of a

time.
man.
Maybe all I want is to hold you right now
I'm not a queen in-side a mir-ror no more.

with no com-pro - mise.}
I'm not a god to hold your hand.}
This is the real ___ real ___

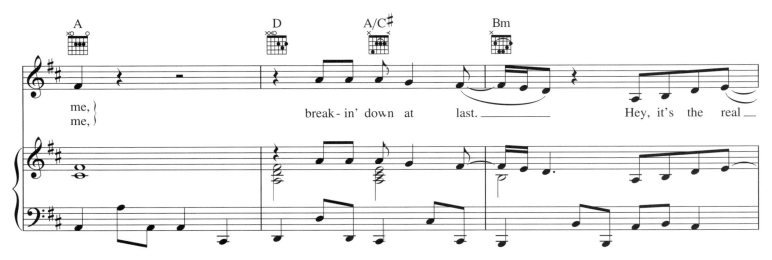

me,}
me,}
break-in' down at last. ___ Hey, it's the real ___

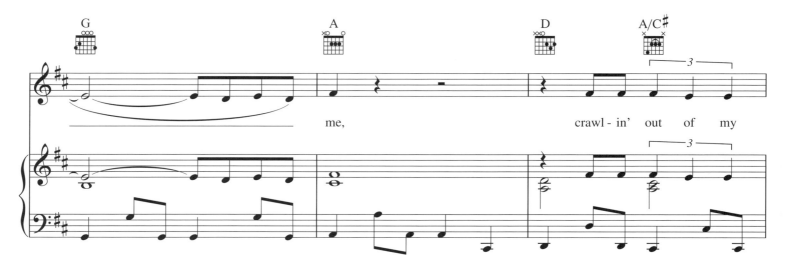

me, crawl - in' out of my

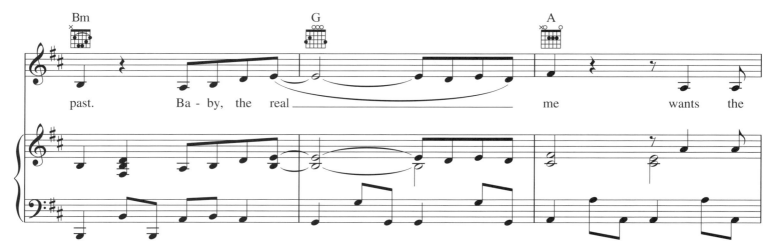

past. Ba - by, the real _____ me wants the

real _____ you so bad.

Well, I've got no an - swers now. _____

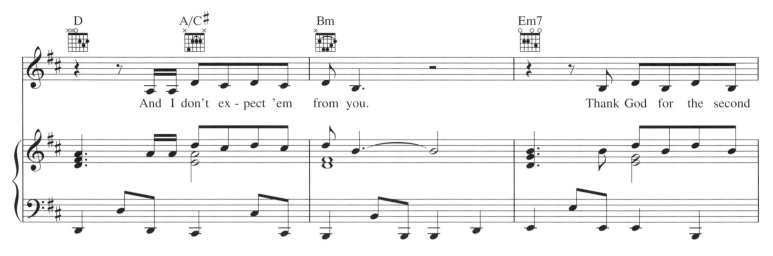

And I don't ex-pect 'em from you.   Thank God for the second

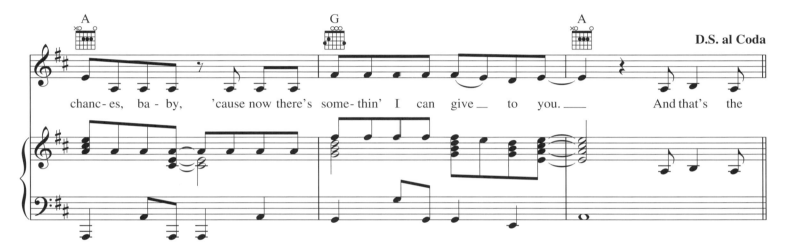

chanc-es, ba-by, 'cause now there's some-thin' I can give __ to you. __   And that's the

D.S. al Coda

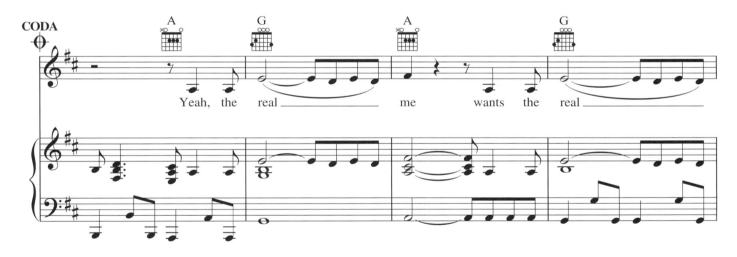

CODA

Yeah, the real _____ me wants the real _____

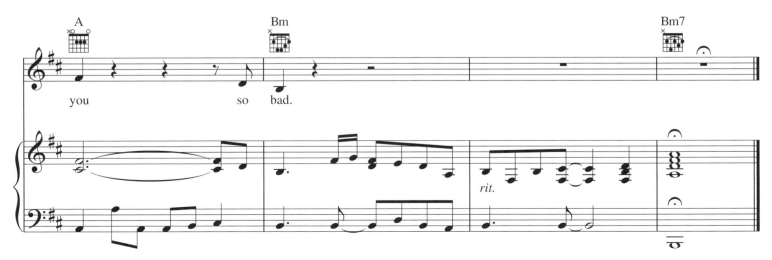

you   so bad.

rit.

RULES OF TRAVEL

Words and Music by ROSANNE CASH
and JOHN LEVENTHAL

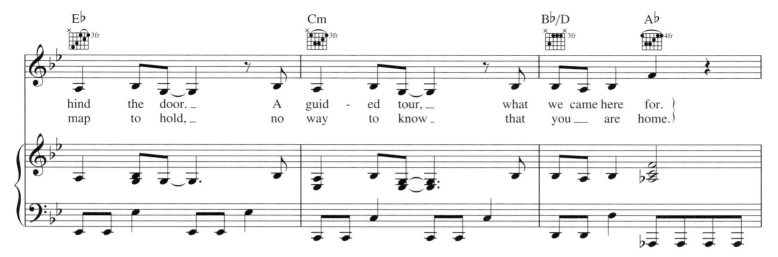

hind the door. _ A guid - ed tour, _ what we came here for.
map to hold, _ no way to know _ that you _ are home.

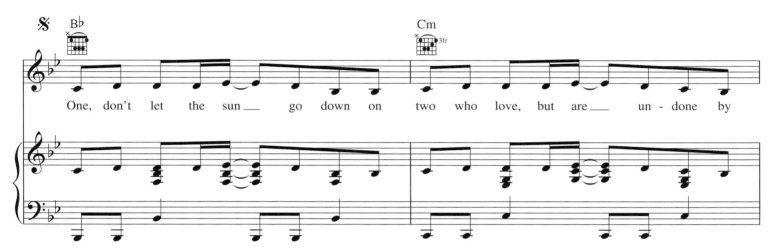

One, don't let the sun _ go down on two who love, but are _ un - done by

three whose name is... I won't e - ven start _ be - fore _ we learn _ the rules. _ Like

one, don't let the sun _ go down on two who love, but are _ un - done by

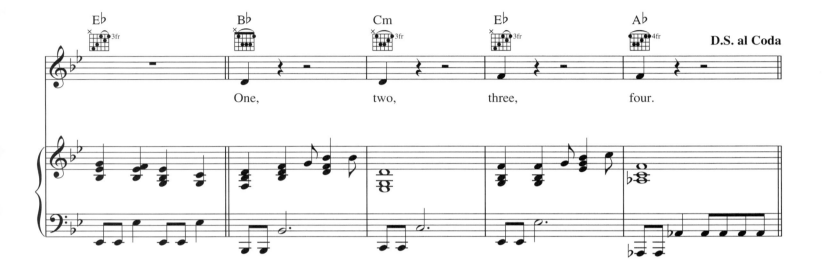

One, two, three, four.

D.S. al Coda

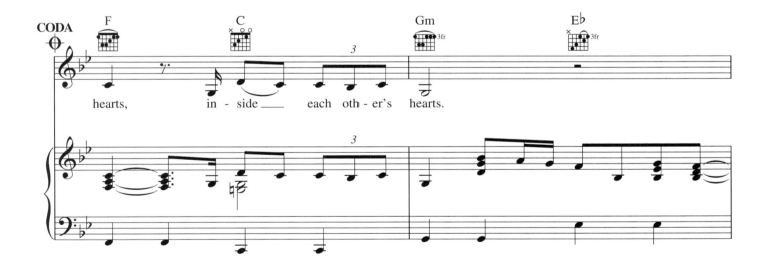

hearts, in - side ___ each oth - er's hearts.

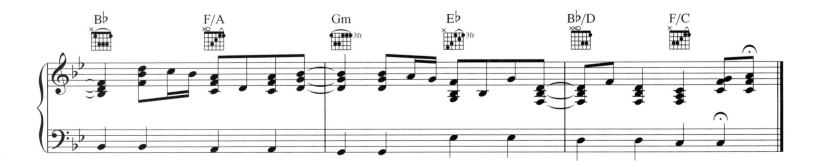

© Courtesy of Rosanne Cash's personal collection.

SEPTEMBER WHEN IT COMES

Words and Music by ROSANNE CASH
and JOHN LEVENTHAL

Moderately

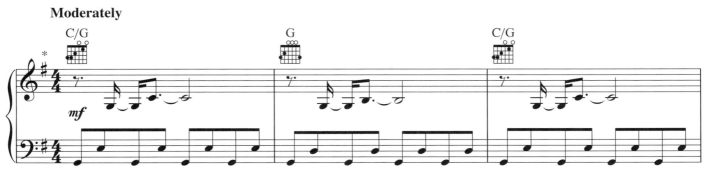

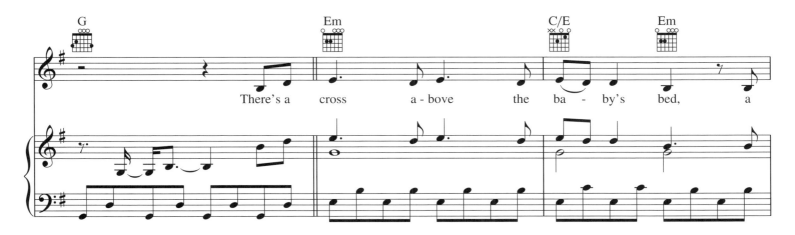

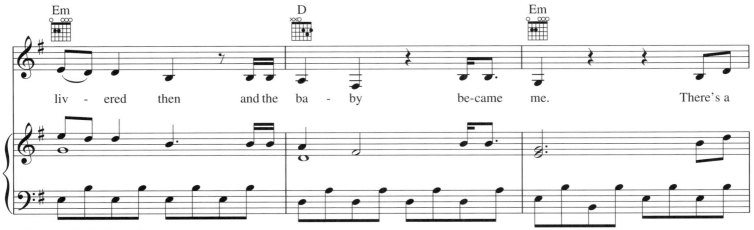

* Recorded a half step lower.

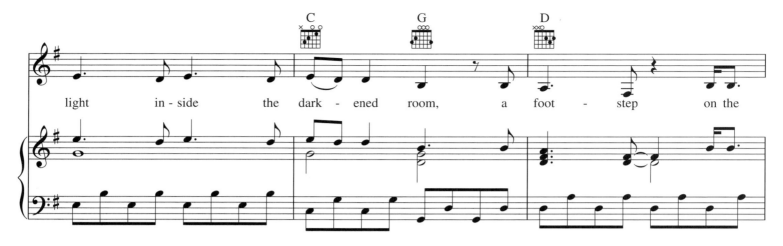

light in-side the dark-ened room, a foot-step on the

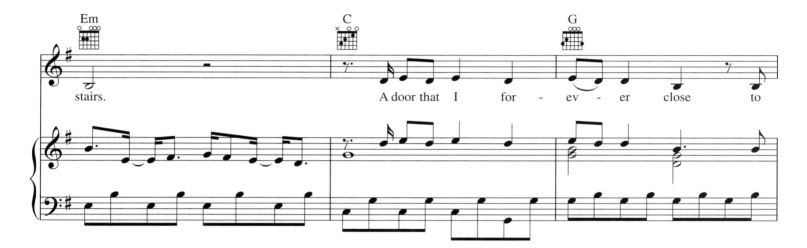

stairs. A door that I for-ev-er close to

leave those mem'ries there.

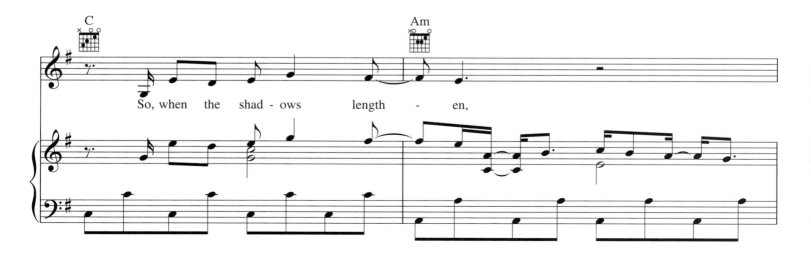

So, when the shad-ows length-en,

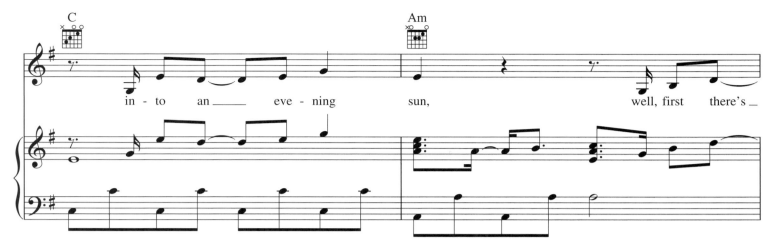

in - to an ___ eve - ning sun, well, first there's ___

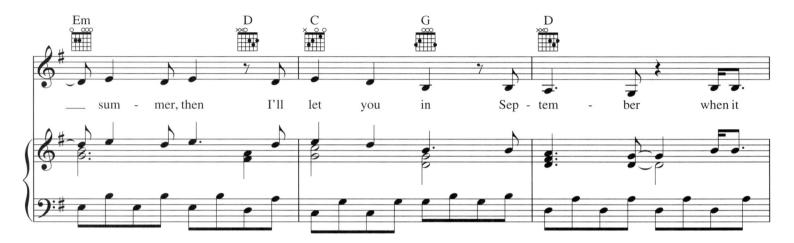

___ sum - mer, then I'll let you in Sep - tem - ber when it

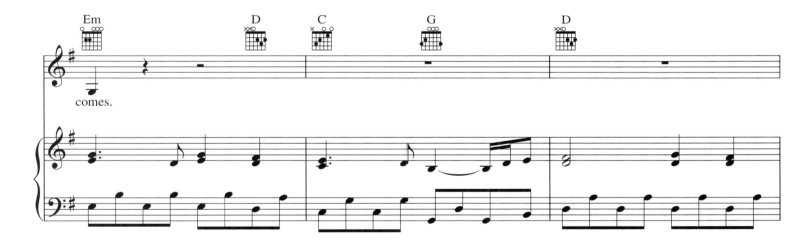

comes.

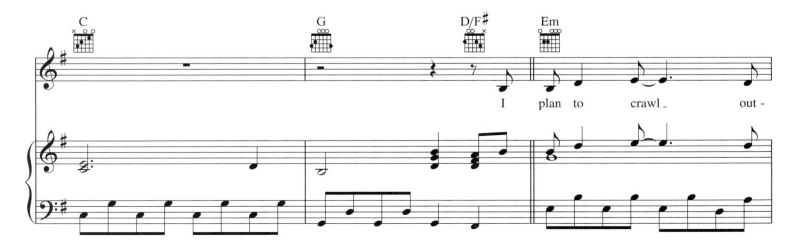

I plan to crawl ___ out -

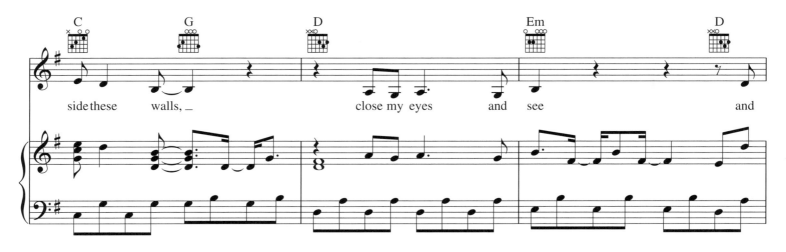

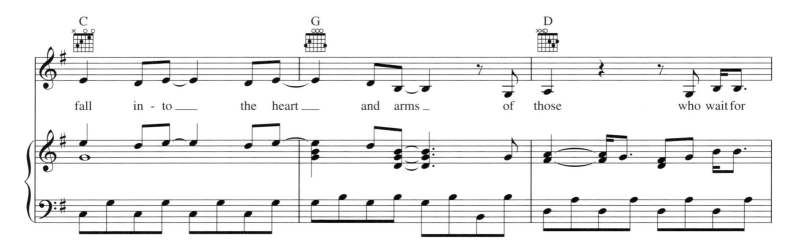

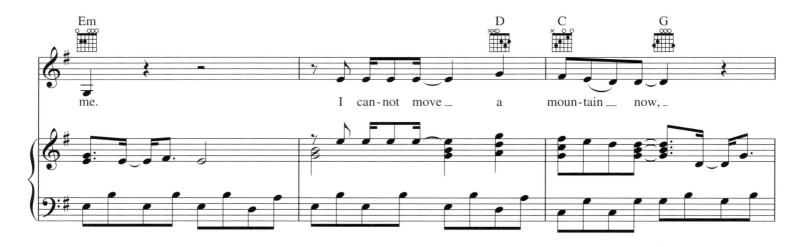

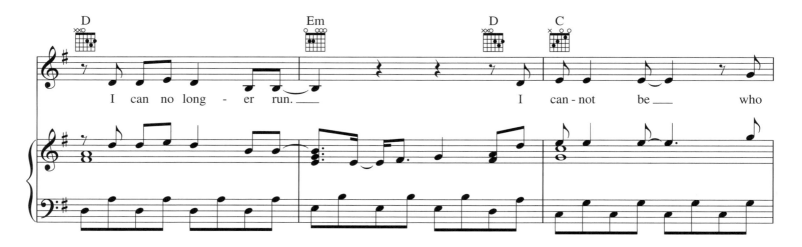

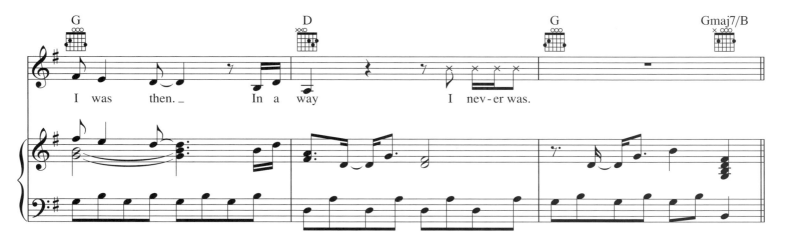

I was then. ___ In a way I nev-er was.

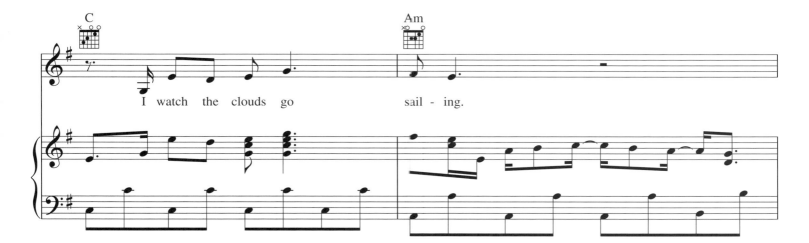

I watch the clouds go sail - ing.

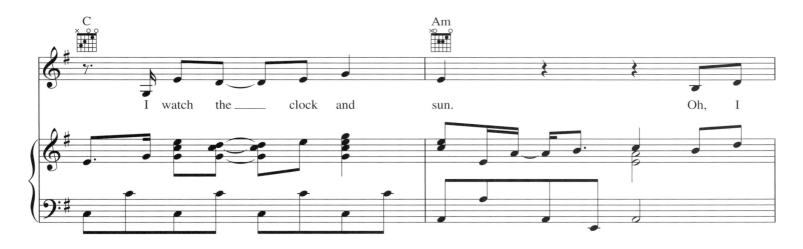

I watch the ___ clock and sun. Oh, I

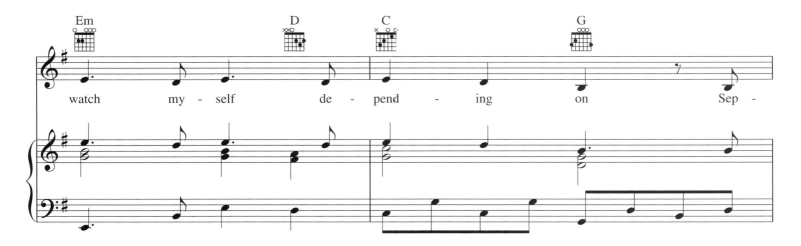

watch my - self de - pend - ing on Sep -

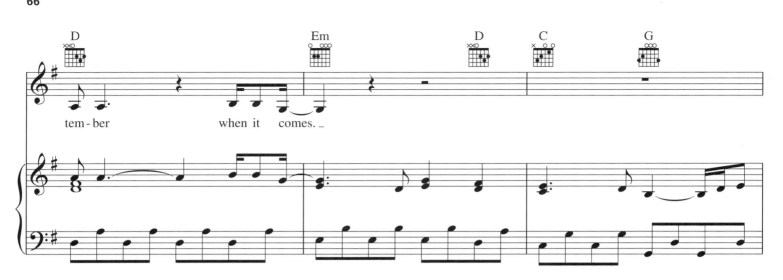

tem - ber   when it   comes. _

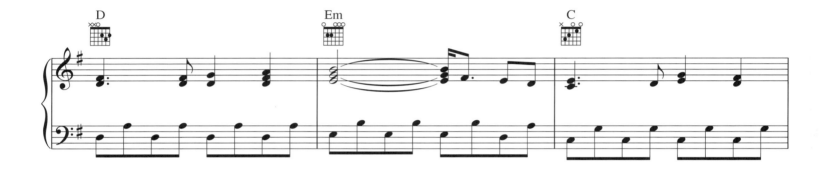

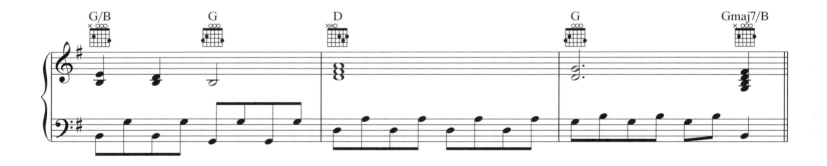

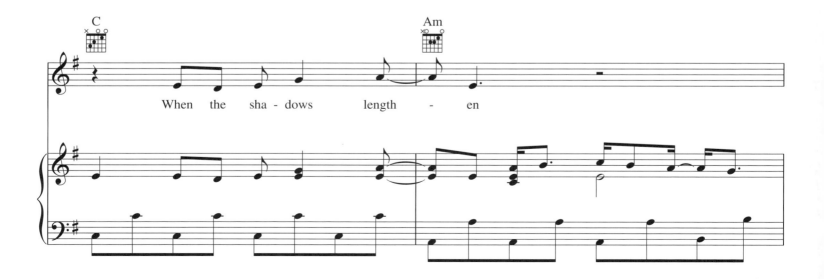

When the sha - dows length - en

and burn a - way the past, _____ they will fly _____

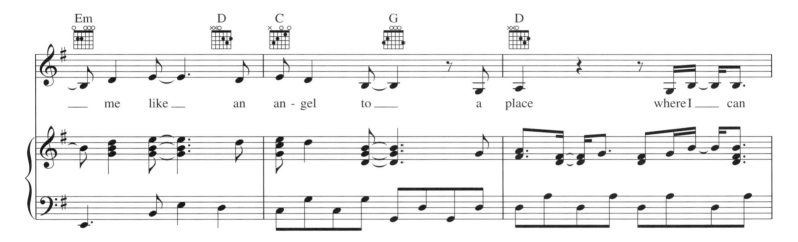

_____ me like _____ an an - gel to _____ a place where I _____ can

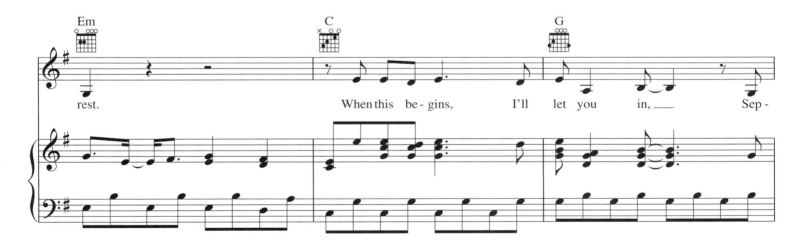

rest. When this be - gins, I'll let you in, _____ Sep -

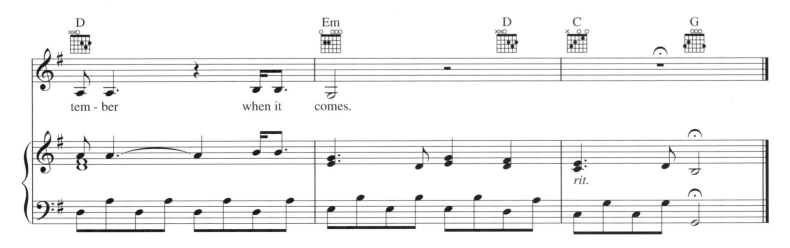

tem - ber when it comes.

SEVEN YEAR ACHE

Words and Music by
ROSANNE CASH

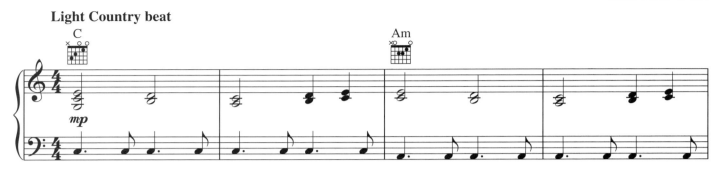

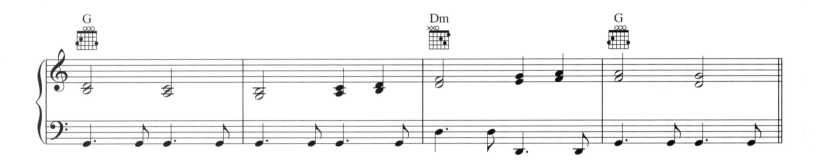

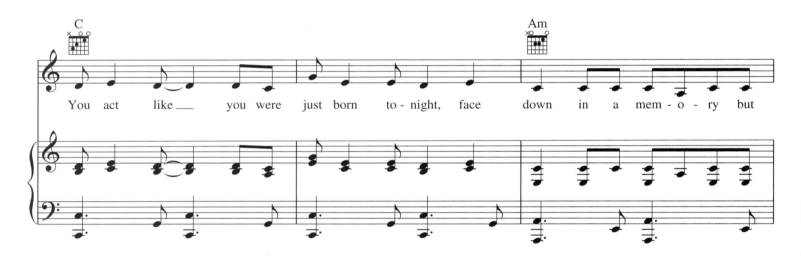

You act like ___ you were just born to-night, face down in a mem-o-ry but

feel-in' all right. ___ So who does your past be-long ___ to to-day, ba-by,

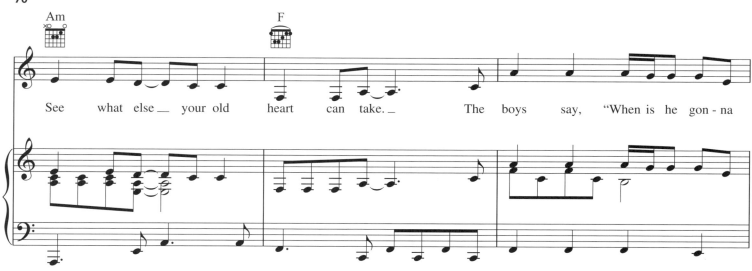

See what else __ your old heart can take. __ The boys say, "When is he gon- na

give us some room," _____ the girls say, "God, I hope he comes back soon." _

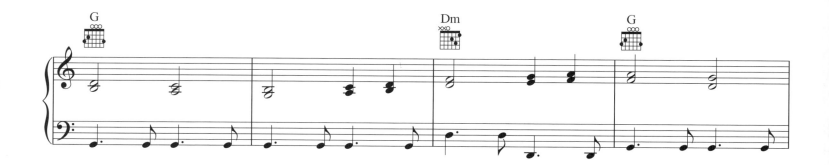

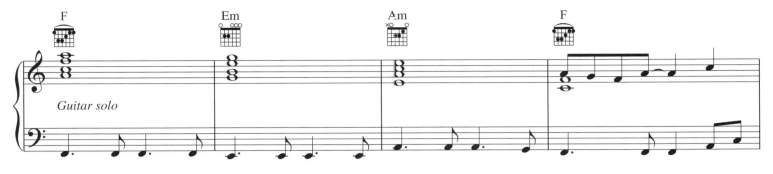

What is so great _ a-bout sleep-in' down-town? _ There's plen-ty of dives _ to be

some-one you're not. _ Just say you're look-in' for some - thin' you might of for-got. _____

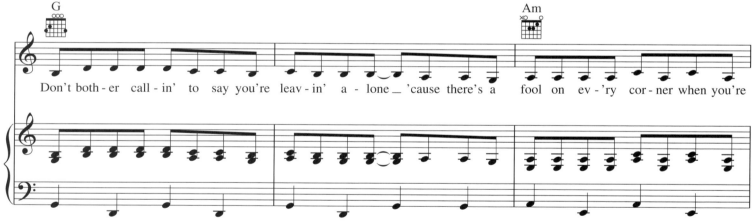

Don't both-er call-in' to say you're leav-in' a - lone _ 'cause there's a fool on ev-'ry cor-ner when you're

try'n' to get home. _ Just tell 'em
               Tell me } you're try - in' to cure a se - ven year ache. _

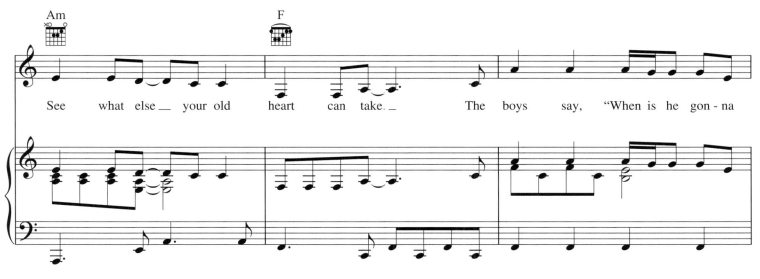

See what else — your old heart can take. — The boys say, "When is he gon-na

give us some room," ——— the girls say, "God, I hope he comes back soon." —

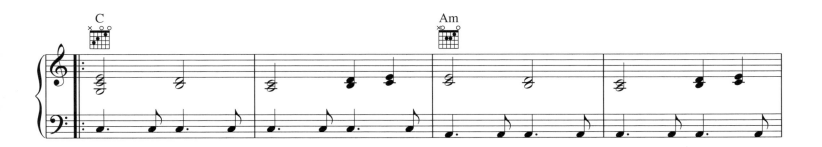

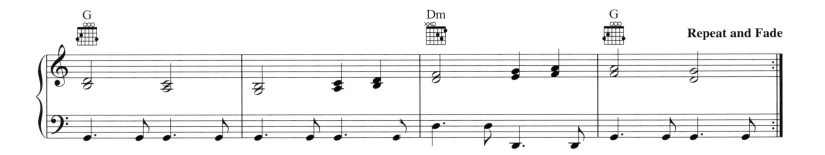

Repeat and Fade

SLEEPING IN PARIS

Words and Music by
ROSANNE CASH

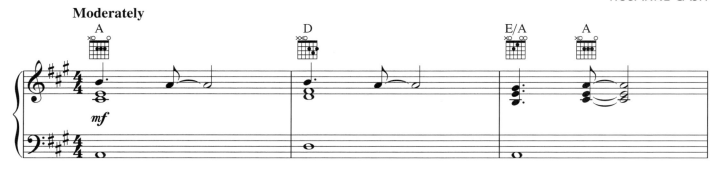

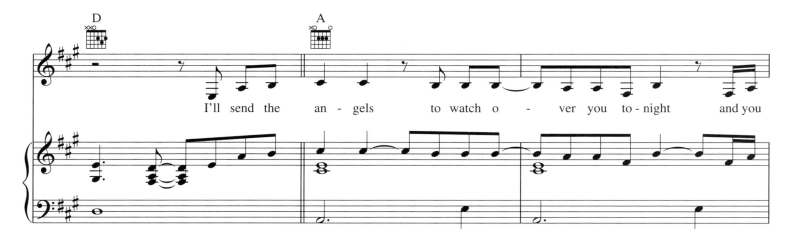

I'll send the an - gels to watch o - ver you to - night and you

send them right __ back to me. __ A lone - ly road is a bod - y-

guard   if we real - ly want it to be.

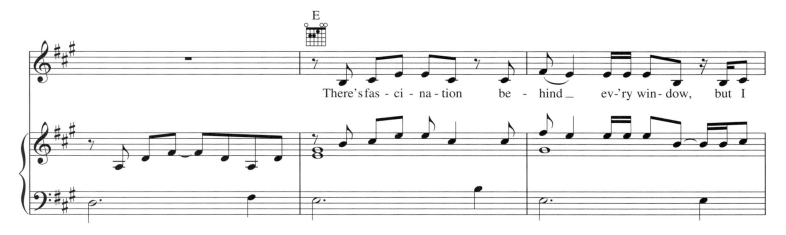

There's fas - ci - na - tion be - hind _ ev-'ry win-dow, but I

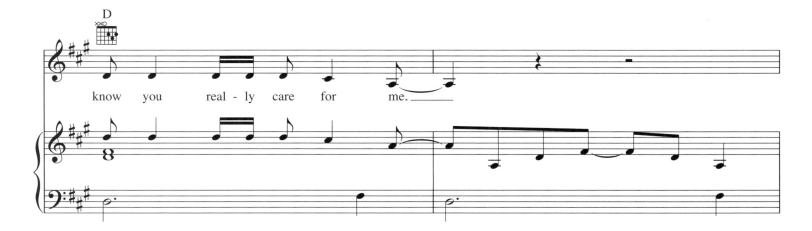

know you real - ly care for me. _

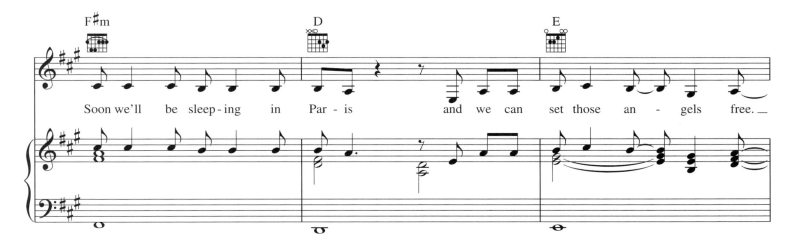

Soon we'll be sleep - ing in Par - is and we can set those an - gels free. _

No one sees be - hind _____ the mask. _

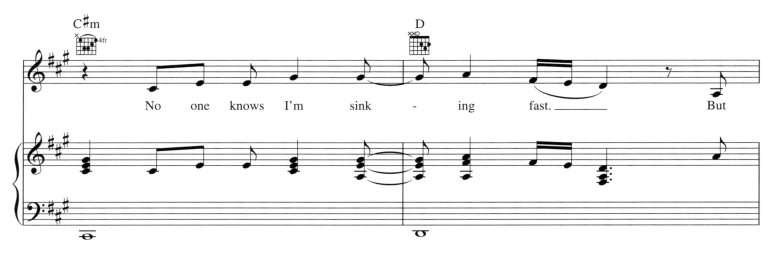

No one knows I'm sink - ing fast. _____ But

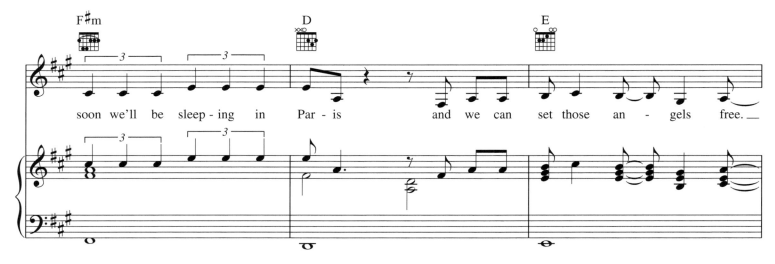

soon we'll be sleep - ing in Par - is and we can set those an - gels free. _____

Love is just an - oth - er slave,

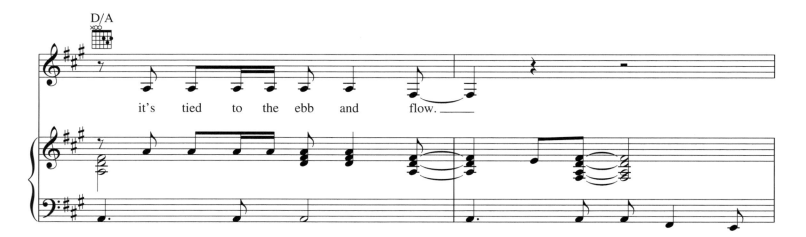

it's tied to the ebb and flow. _____

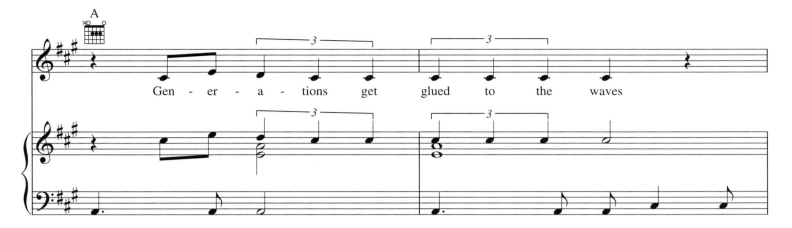

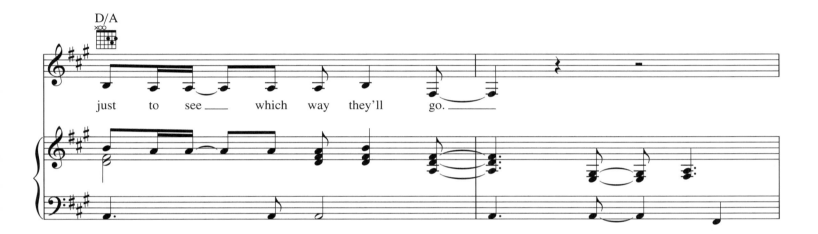

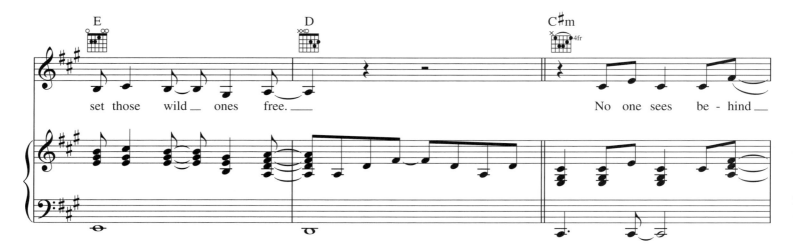

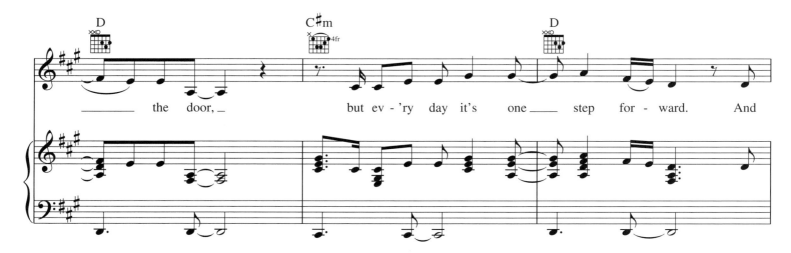

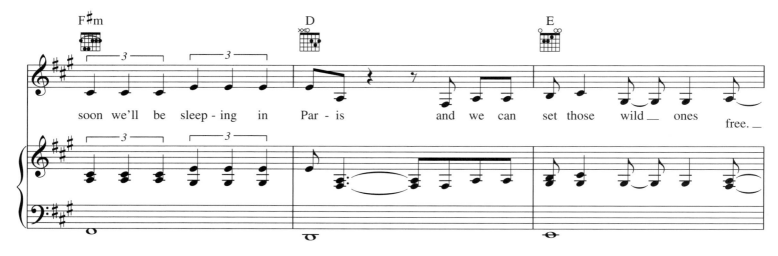

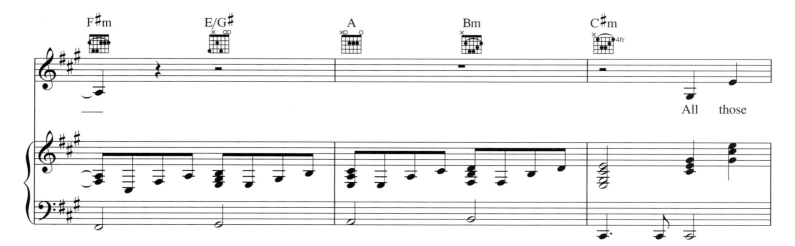

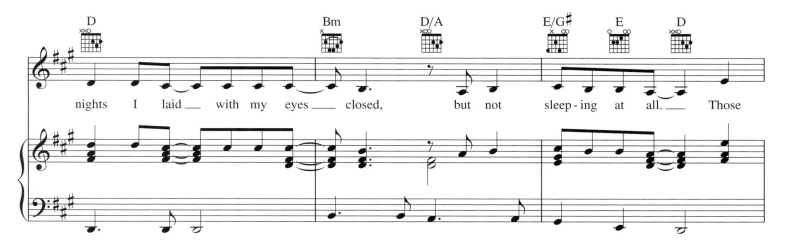

nights I laid ___ with my eyes ___ closed, but not sleep-ing at all. ___ Those

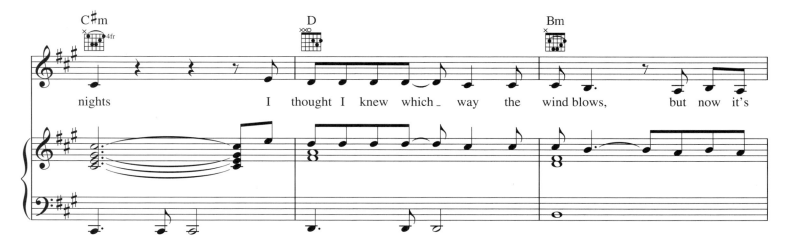

nights I thought I knew which ___ way the wind blows, but now it's

blow-ing me back to you. ___ The wind speaks French,

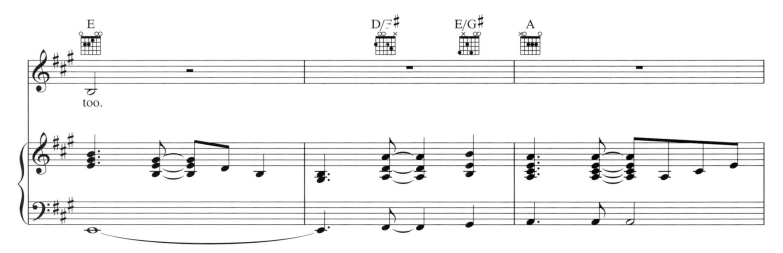

too.

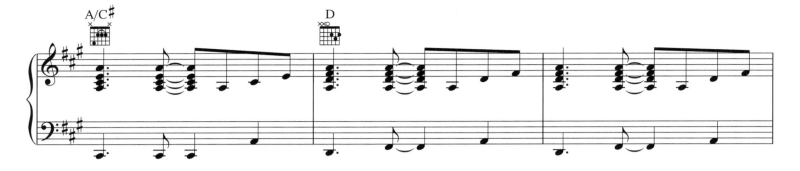

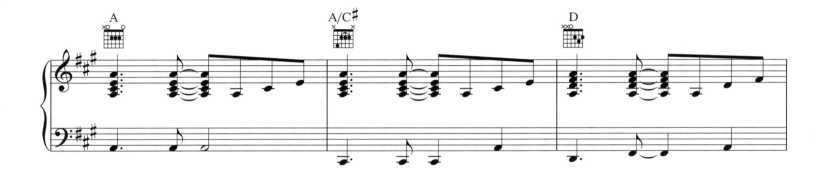

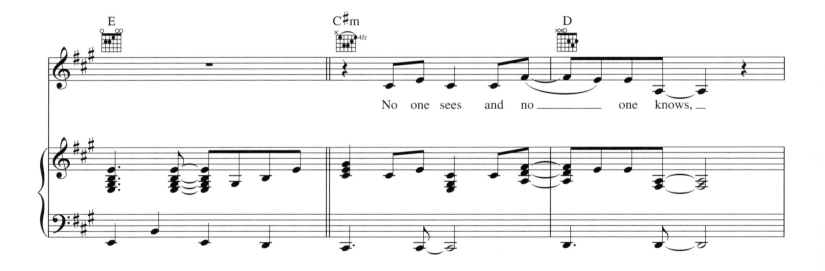

No one sees and no _____ one knows, _____

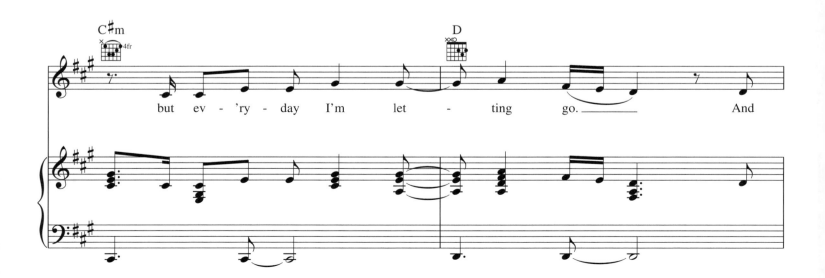

but ev - 'ry - day I'm let - ting go. _____ And

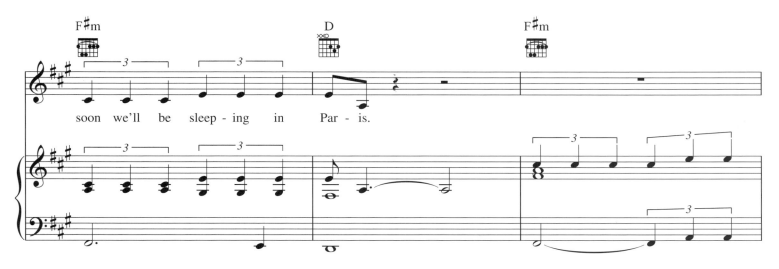

soon we'll be sleep - ing in Par - is.

Soon we'll be sleep - ing in Par - is and we can

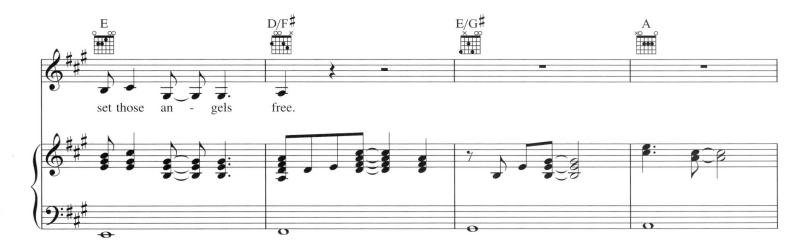

set those an - gels free.

rit.

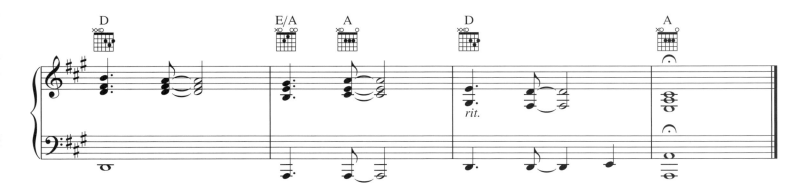

WHAT WE REALLY WANT

Words and Music by
ROSANNE CASH

We tried to make our - selves
I wan - na call out your
We are ships in the
We tried to make it feel

pay ___ for some-thing we've nev - er done.
name. ___ I wan - na hold out my hand.
night. ___ The wa - ter's deep in be - tween.
right ___ in some - one else - 's world. ___

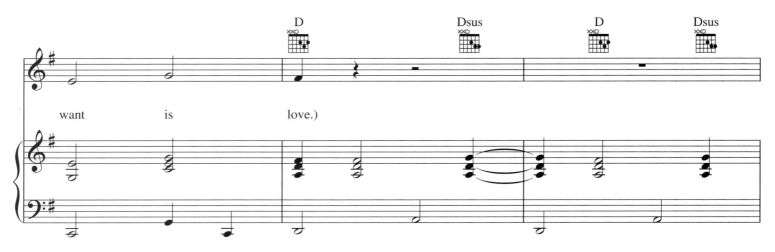

want   is   love.)

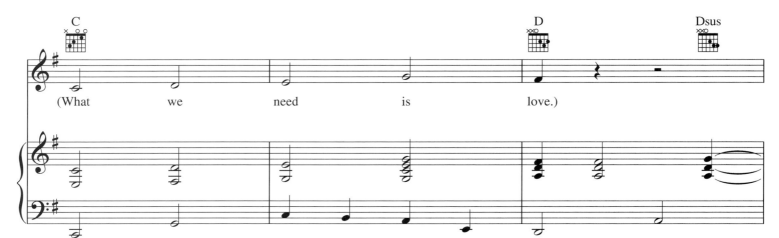

(What   we   need   is   love.)

D.C. al Coda

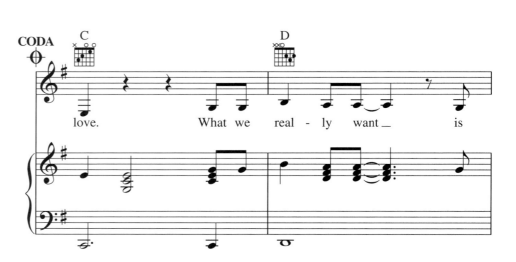

CODA

love.   What we real - ly want ___ is

love.   What we real - ly need ___   is   love   (What   we

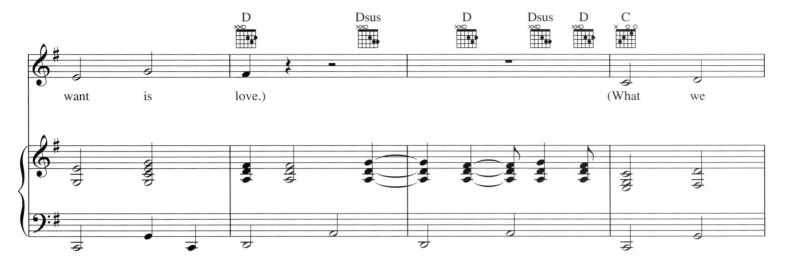

want is love.) (What we

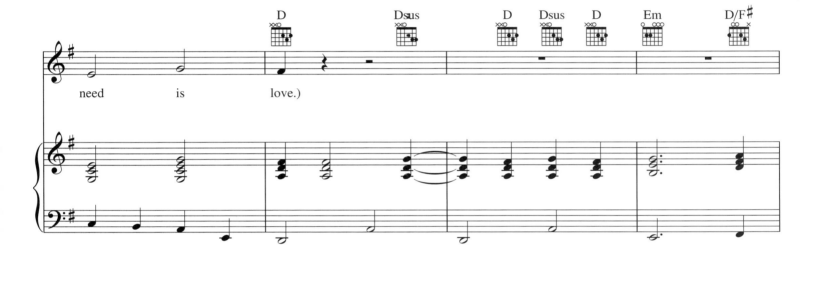

need is love.)

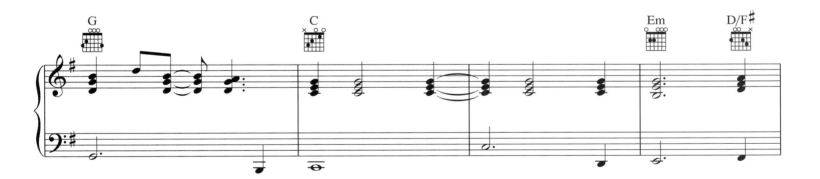

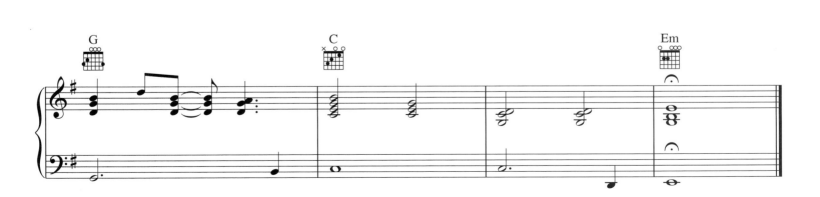

THE WORLD UNSEEN

Words and Music by
ROSANNE CASH

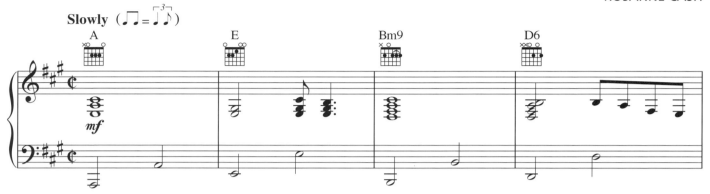

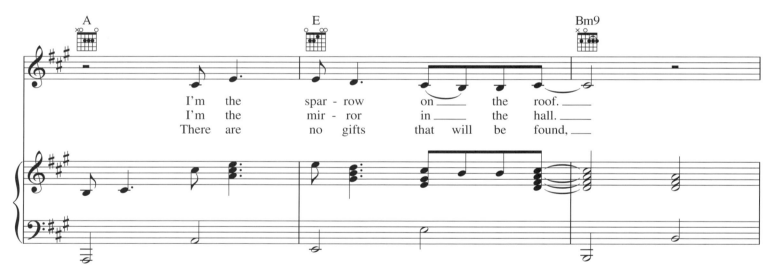

I'm the spar - row on the roof.
I'm the mir - ror in the hall.
There are no gifts that will be found,

I'm the list of ev - 'ry -
From your emp - ty room
wrapped in win - ter, laid be -

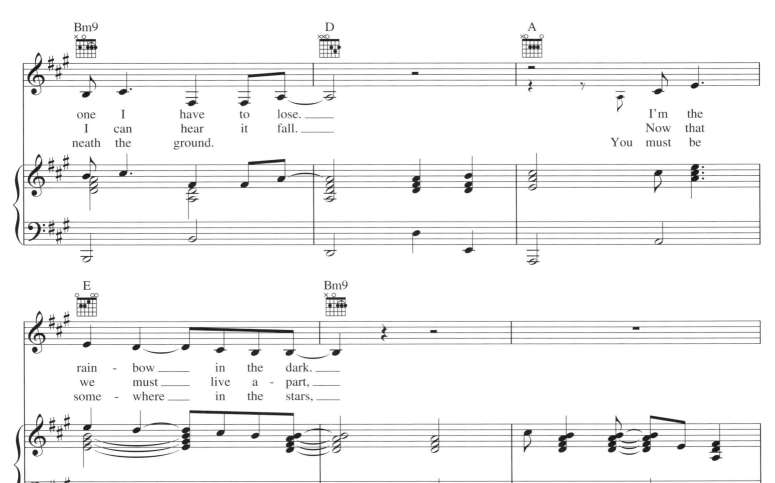

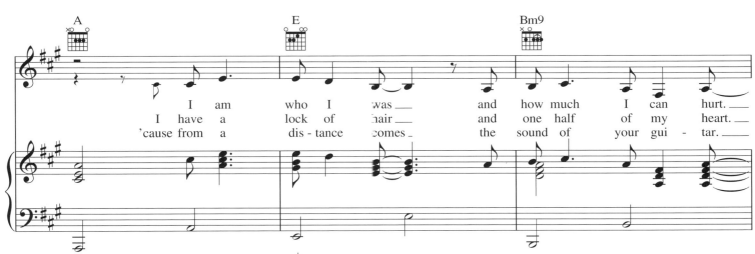

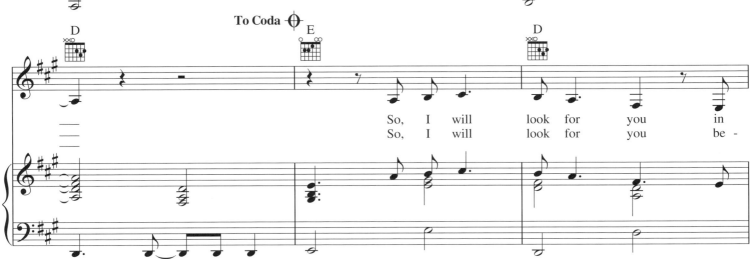

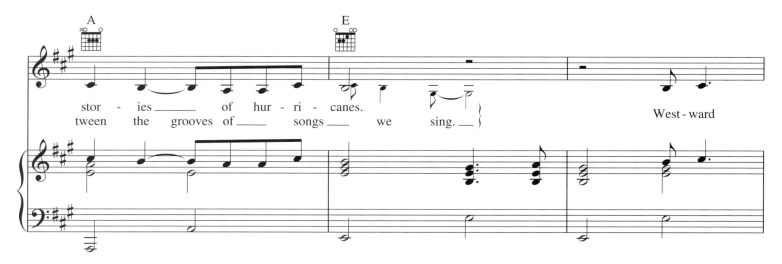

stories ____ of hur - ri - canes.
tween the grooves of ____ songs ____ we sing. ____
West - ward

lead - ing, still pro - ceed - ing to the world ____ un - seen. ____

D.C. al Coda

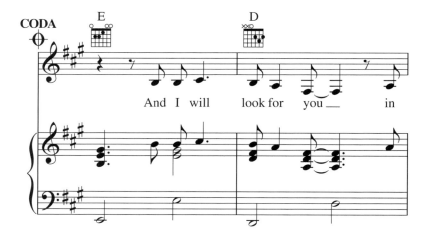

CODA

And I will look for you ____ in

Mem - phis ____ and the miles ____ be - tween. ____
I will

look for you___ in mor-phine___ and in dreams.___ I will

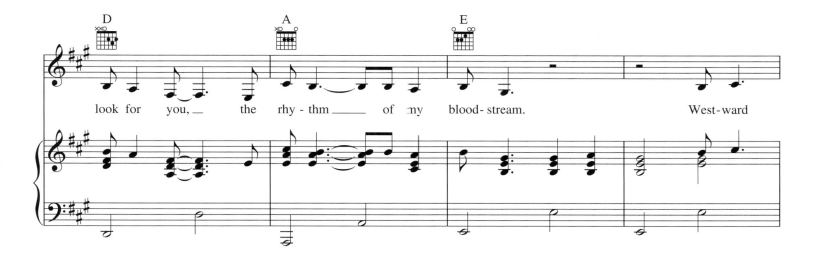

look for you,___ the rhy-thm___ of my blood-stream. West-ward

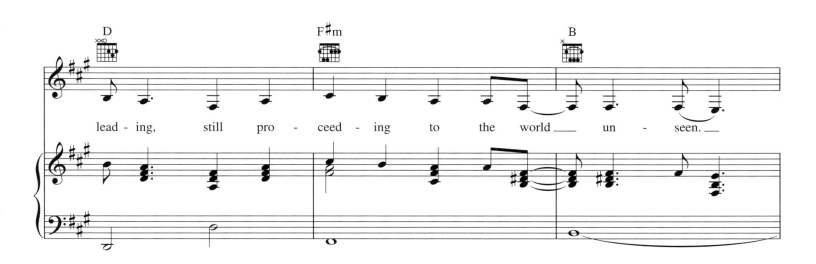

lead-ing, still pro-ceed-ing to the world___ un - seen.___

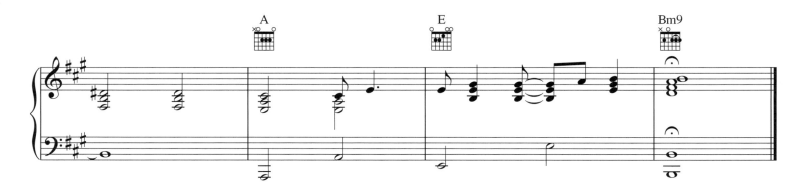

THE WHEEL

Words and Music by
ROSANNE CASH

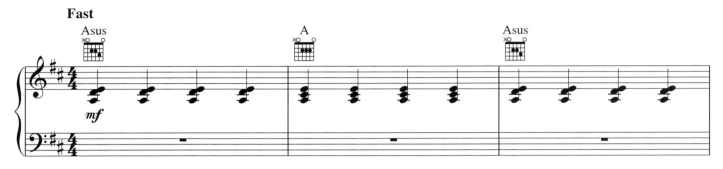

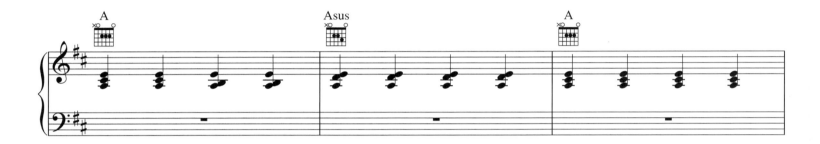

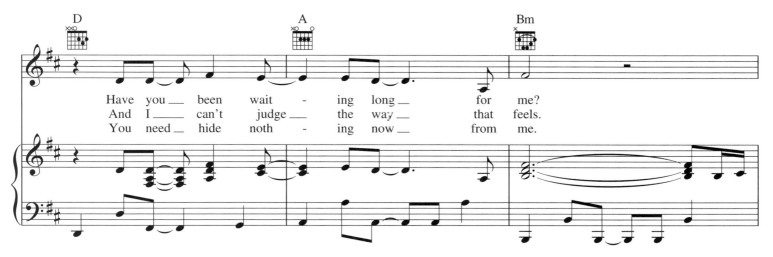

Have you ___ been wait - ing long ___ for me?
And I ___ can't judge ___ the way ___ that feels.
You need ___ hide noth - ing now ___ from me.

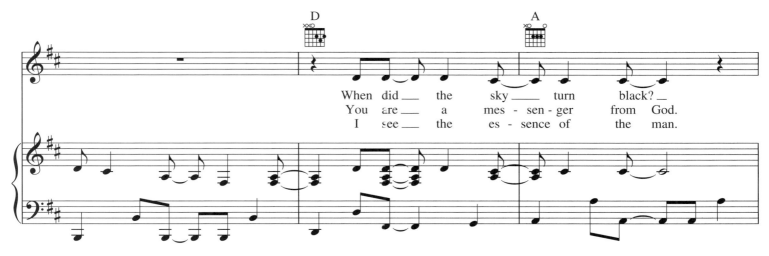

When did ___ the sky ___ turn black? ___
You are ___ a mes - sen - ger from God.
I see ___ the es - sence of the man.

Do you ___ still want ___ me back? ___
You are ___ the an - gel I for - got.
I stand ___ be - fore ___ you as a friend.

I'll pick it all ___
And I can't say ___
The truth moves through ___

___ up piece by piece.
___ it is - n't real.
___ us e - ven when we sleep.

And the wheel ___

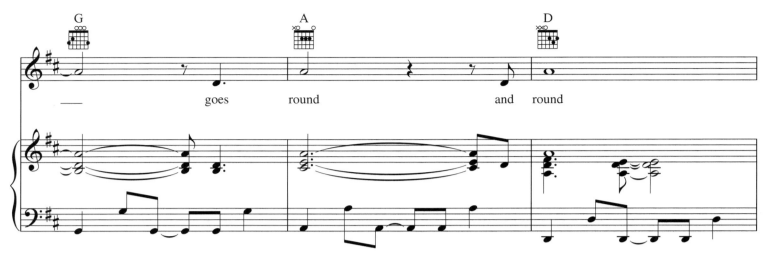

goes round   and round

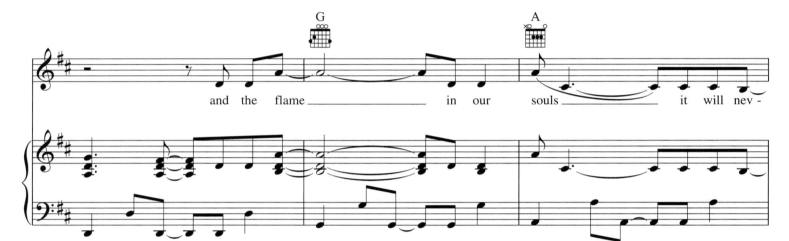

and the flame _____ in our souls _____ it will nev-

-er burn __ out.   And the wheel, __   and the wheel __

To Coda ⊕

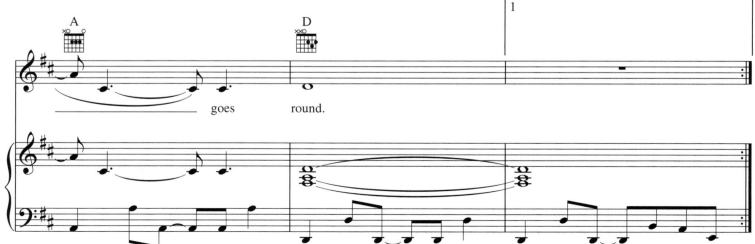

_____ goes round.

1

Well, I'm not look-in' for ___ your

an - swers. Oh, dar -

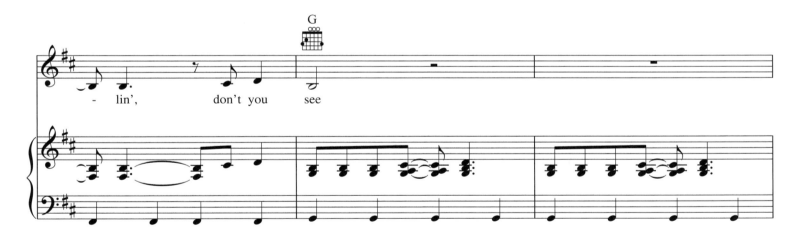

- lin', don't you see

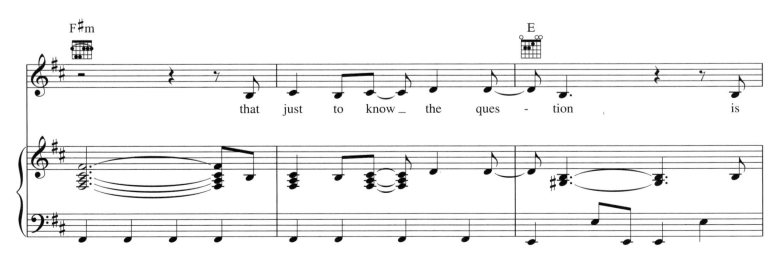

that just to know ___ the ques - tion is

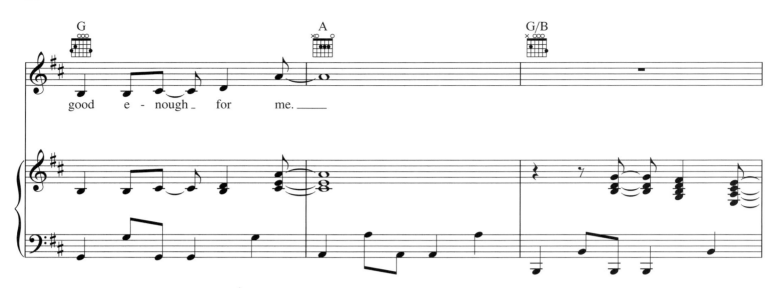

good e - nough for me. _____

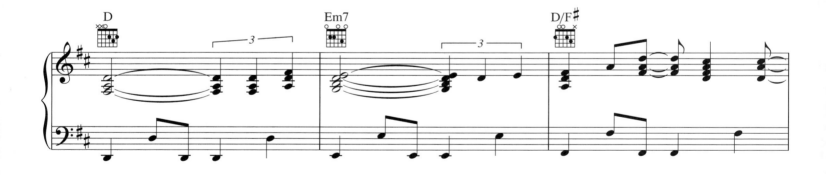

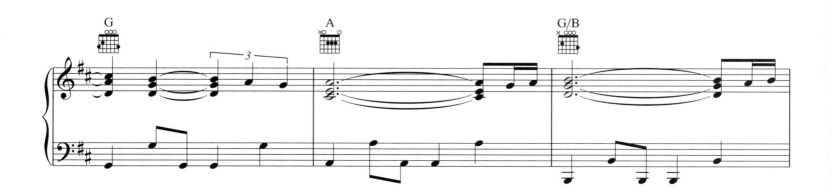

D.S. al Coda

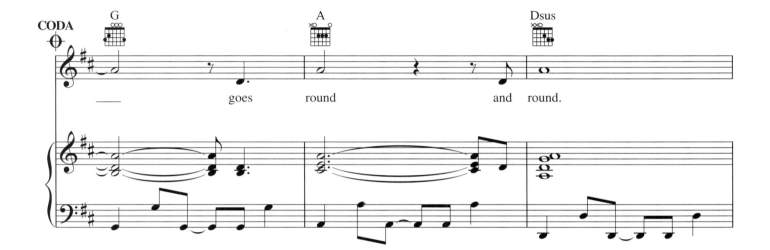

CODA

goes round and round.

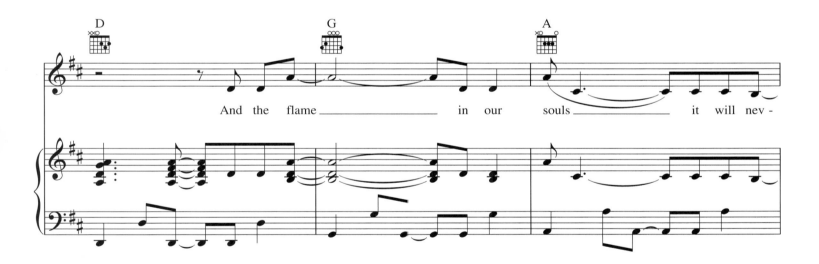

And the flame _____ in our souls _____ it will nev-

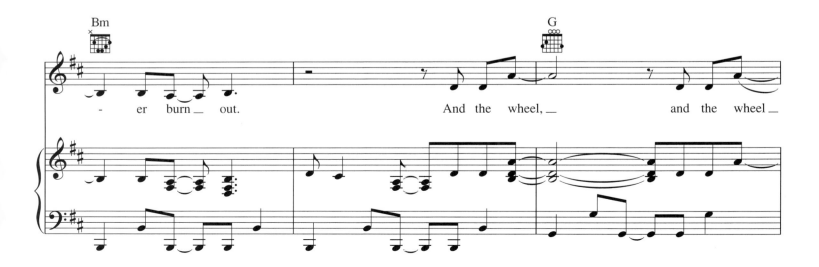

-er burn __ out. And the wheel, __ and the wheel __

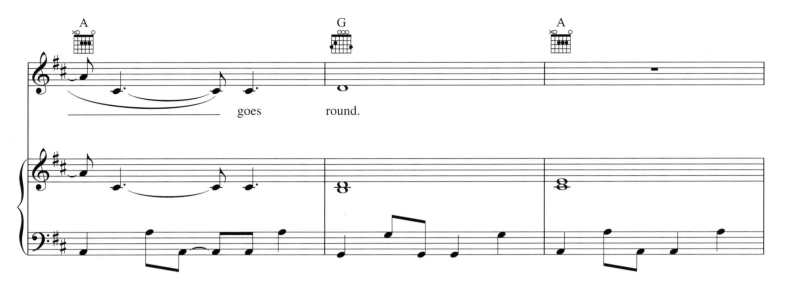

goes round.

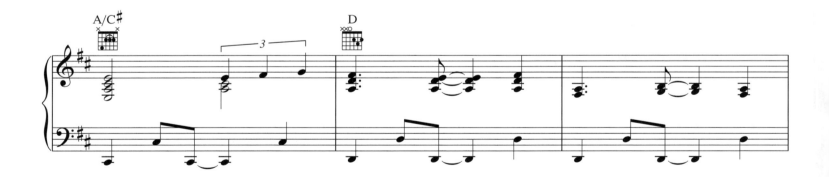